GUIDE TO PRAYER & MEDITATION

1ST EDITION

How to Love, Honor, and Respect
Ourselves

Selah סלה

Table of Contents

1ˢᵗ Edition

Author's Note

Our purpose in life is to love, honor,
respect ourselves, and be drawn into a
relationship with a God of one's
understanding.

With this relationship of Divine Awareness,
we begin to thrive, overcome adversity, and
help others while honoring ourselves.

About This Book

In the 11th Step, "We sought prayer and meditation to improve our conscious contact with a higher power or God of our understanding."

This book offers nonsectarian prayers and meditations to assist 12-step program newcomers and old-timers in rekindling their relationship with a higher power and gaining self-love. The book also provides examples of generational and ancestral healing with notions of quantum entanglement.

We use "Selah" interchangeably as a proper noun and a verb that means "to pause and reflect."

Divine Awareness refers to our Higher Power, the God of our understanding, well-being, happiness, and peace of mind. The term also refers to our willingness to protect the well-being, happiness, and peace of mind of others, whether friend or foe.

In Part I of this book, we share stories from people who overcame extreme hardship to embrace Divine Awareness in a rewarding and joyful life that includes giving to others.

In Part II, we introduce the Ego-self, Satan, and the Inner Child, stimulating the need for introspection, meditation, and prayer.

In Part III, we introduce the concept of meditation as a form of mindful bathing and self-care. Examples of meditation are provided.

In Part IV, we introduce prayers of healing and blessings to heal our inner selves and pray for the Divine blessing of others.

Selected Quotes

"The past cannot be changed. But the past can change you for the better, or it can change you for the worse. My question is, why not make it for the better?" ~ *Jocko Willink, Retired Navy Seal Commander*

"You don't blame people for having unconscious patterns. You try to make them conscious of it." ~ *Gabor Maté*

"We do have a choice in how we respond. And to curl up in a ball and feel sorry for yourself or blame it on somebody else isn't going to change it. You've got to get up, you've got to make a choice, and you've got to move forward." ~ *Debbie "Momma" Lee* – *Gold Star Mother*

"Therefore, confess to one another your sense of being helpless and powerless and pray for each other that you may be healed." ~ *James 5:16*

"These two young fish are swimming along, and they happen to meet an older fish swimming the other way, who nods at them and says, "Morning, boys. How's the water?" And the two young fish swim on for a bit, and then eventually, one of them looks over at the other and goes, "What the hell is water?" ~ *David Foster Wallace*

"It's best not to speak your opinion of someone else's sin unless you know how they arrived there." ~ *Pastor John Gray.*

"A loving touch on the arm is better than a false orgasm." ~ Richard Rohr, OFM

"Addiction emerges from a lack of inner experience of intimacy with oneself, God, life, and the moment. One helpful clarification is that many addicts confuse intensity with intimacy, just as most young people do with noise, artificial highs, and overstimulation." ~ Richard Rohr from his book Breathing Under Water: Spirituality and the Twelve Steps.

"I often say that if I had a prayer, it would be this: God, spare me from the desire for love, approval, or appreciation. Amen." " I don't have a prayer, of course, because I don't want anything but what I have." ~ Byron Katie from her book Loving What Is, Revised Edition: Four Questions That Can Change Your Life.

"It is at the bottom of life we must begin and not at the top, nor should we permit our grievances to overshadow our opportunities." ~ Booker T. Washington, from his book "Up From Slavery."

Divine Awareness

"The clouds, they are like the thoughts, but the thoughts they can only appear, or the clouds can only appear because the underlying "big" is the sky.

"So, there are clouds in the sky. There are images of the movie on the screen, and emotions come up on behalf of your existing perception.

"So that means what you have, what we all have, is what we are able to perceive. And some people, based on something that is triggering them, sometimes perceive anger coming up; they perceive sadness coming up.

"So, these emotional states, they can be perceived. If they can be perceived, then it means they are not you because you are the one who sees them.

"And non-identification means that you can witness that these things are like clouds that sometimes pop up in the sky, and just like every cloud on this earth, neither of these clouds ever stays. It's only sometimes a sequence, an episode, within your lifetime. And this idea of non-identification is related to this direction.

"Yeah, meaning that you understand that you see why this fear came up with what it is related to and ultimately also see that there is no substance to it."

"Greatest Advice" from Shaolin master Shi Heng Yi's– *When You Feel Like Giving Up;* Mulligan Brothers on YouTube.

To learn more about awareness from the perspective of a Buddhist monk, lookup "How to Tap into Your Awareness" by Yongey Mingyur Rinpoche, or click here: for his lovely TED Talk.

Also, see or read the Tao Te Ching, a classical Chinese text attributed to the legendary philosopher Laozi. It is one of the most important works in Chinese philosophy and is considered the foundational text of Taoism.

The Tao Te Ching consists of 81 short chapters or verses that offer wisdom and insights into the Tao, often translated as "the Way." The Tao is the ultimate reality, an ineffable force that pervades all things and guides the universe. According to the Tao Te Ching, the Way cannot be described in words but can only be experienced directly.

The text is concise and poetic, using paradoxical language and metaphor to convey its message. It offers guidance on how to live in harmony with the Tao and achieve balance, simplicity, and humility.

The Tao Te Ching has been translated into many languages and has influenced many philosophical and spiritual traditions, including Taoism, Buddhism, Confucianism, and Western philosophy.

Part I

Jonny's Story

Forgiving a Parent

As a child, Jonny Kim tried valiantly to protect his mother and brother from their violent, verbally abusive, and alcoholic father, who owned a liquor store, of all things. One day, Jonny wanted to fight back, but his father sprayed mace in Jonny's face and tried to crush his skull with a barbell. Afterward, while his father hid in the attic, Jonny called the police, who later shot his father, killing him. Jonny says he felt "a huge weight coming off my shoulders" as the years of abuse ended.

Jonny's story would be compelling enough if he survived without "becoming his father," as many do. Instead, we have one of the most compelling stories of self-care, knowledge, teamwork, self-discipline, and leadership.

The Rake, Issue #71

"Dr. Jonny Kim [became] a former Navy Seal, a veteran of two combat deployments and more than 100 sorties, for which he was awarded the Silver and Bronze Star medals, with a citation for valor; he won a scholarship to, and graduated from, Harvard medical school; and he is NASA's first Korean-

American astronaut, who at the age of 35 has achieved far more than most of us will ever dream of achieving in our entire lives.

"But his reaction to the abuse he suffered in childhood and his decision to become a protector of humanity rather than a perpetrator of its often seemingly inevitable cycle of inherited behavior is most admirable.

"My father had many demons like many people. I think he did his best to live those demons, but he often didn't have the mental strength not to let those demons get hold." ~ *Dr. Jonny Kim*

Jonny Kim's interview is available on Jocko Podcast #221

Jonny Kim's story with pictures is available in Issue #71 of The Rake.

Kirstie's Story

Forgiving God

"A helicopter crash on June 23rd, 2012, was the defining moment in my life. I suffered a broken spine and damaged my upper arms. I remember screaming with tears rolling down my face when they said they would take my leg above the knee."

"I thought it was all over and that my dreams were turned into nightmares. I have it on repeat in my head, a scream encompassing terror, pain, and fear of what my life would become." ~ *Kirstie Ennis*

From the Kirstie Ennis Foundation website:

"Kirstie Ennis's story may have begun when she lost her leg after her helicopter went down in Afghanistan, but it certainly doesn't end there. After more than 40 surgeries and the amputation of her leg, first below and then above the knee after a life-threatening infection, the former Marine sergeant has accomplished more at 28 than most people have achieved in a lifetime.

"Ennis' story has been well-documented. She allowed cameras into the hospital to film her amputation ordeal for an inspired short

film produced by Cosmopolitan magazine."
"She was featured on the cover of ESPN
magazine for the "Body" issue. Photos of
Prince Harry embracing Ennis after she
completed the 1,000-mile walk across
England, Wales, and Scotland for the British
non-profit Walking for the Wounded appeared
in People magazine, and she was later
honored by the magazine as their "Annual
Body Image Hero" in 2016.

"Ennis has turned the concept of "disabled
athlete" on its head, proving how capable she
still is, whether it's on one leg or two. She
competed in boardercross and banked slalom
as a Paralympic snowboarder and then
ventured into mountaineering, summitting
Mt Kilimanjaro (at 19,341 feet, it's the
highest point in Africa) to support the non-
profit The Waterboys; then successfully
climbed Carstenzs, the highest point in
Oceania, for The Heroes Project; and then
conquered Iliniza Norte, a 16,818-foot peak in
Ecuador. She has attempted Cotopaxi, the
highest peak in Ecuador, got turned around
by weather on Denali, and made it to the
South Summit of Everest. She hopes to
complete the Seven Summits by climbing the
highest peak on every continent by 2021.

"What people might not know about Ennis:
she's completed three master's degrees
(Human Behavior, Business Administration,

and Public Administration) and is currently working on completing her doctorate in Education. She worked as a stuntwoman on "Patriots Day" starring Mark Wahlberg in 2016. She's a motivational speaker and appeared on stage at Madison Square Garden in 2015 during the New York Comedy Arts Festival for the Bob Woodruff Foundation's 9th Annual Stand Up for Heroes Event. She's an entrepreneur and businesswoman who launched a t-shirt apparel company, HeadCase, and opened her first business, the Chapter One Hair and Body Lab, in Oceanside, California, in 2017. She recently earned her license as a real estate broker for Engel & Volkers in Aspen, Colorado.

Kirstie's Mantras:

"Reflect on who you are and what you have to offer. Give more than you get."

"There are no boundaries – we want to help all people, not just one category (i.e., veterans, disabled, kids, women)."

"Show the world that we control our circumstances, and they do not control us."

"The intention is to go beyond the Seven Summits/Grand Slam, for example, swim the English Channel or do the Seven Volcanoes."

"The reason for the non-profit is to distribute funds evenly – for example, Everest, a big, sexy mountain, will raise the most funds. It isn't fair to other non-profits to be dedicated to smaller mountains."

Kirstie Ennis' fascinating interview is available on Jocko Podcast #199

Kirstie Ennis' story with pictures is available on the Who is Kirstie Ennis website.

Sue's Story

Forgiving a Child

In her book, <u>A Mother's Reckoning</u>, Sue Klebold spends most of the 280 pages describing her continued love for her son and how she was and remained completely dumbfounded by his horrific act of murder and suicide as one of the two shooters at Columbine High School on April 20, 1999. On page 31, she ends the chapter by saying to her son and God, "How could you? How could you do this?" In other words, fear, with its endless, myriad forms, had settled within her body, mind, and soul.

Throughout the book, Sue mentions that her unending feelings of anger, grief, and overwhelming feelings of self-pity (not the horrendous events that befell her) became the harbingers of her downfall, just as sure as a gunshot.

The narrator states: "For the last sixteen years, Sue Klebold, Dylan's mother, has lived with the indescribable grief and shame of that day." She came to realize over the following days, weeks, and months that no matter how much she did not deserve what befell her, she needed to forgive God and to forgive her son not because either deserved it but rather because she deserved to be free of the negativity in her body, mind, and soul.

Thordis' Story

Forgiving a Rapist

At the age of twenty-four, Thordis Elva boarded her plane in Reykjavik, Iceland, to fly to Cape Town, South Africa, to meet with the man who had raped her the day after she had given him her virginity as a sixteen-year-old girl. Initially and over the years that followed, the man, Tom Stranger, had denied to himself and others that a rape had taken place, but with the encouragement of Thordis over the last eight years, he finally admitted what he had done.

Tom's admittance came when Thordis had finally had enough of her bitterness, remorse, anger, and self-pity. She wanted to forgive Tom not because he deserved it but because she deserved to be free of the negativity in her body, mind, and soul.

The story unfolds when Thordis and Tom agree to meet so that her forgiveness and his confession of the truth would replace what was once bitterness and hatred between them. The book is titled *South of Forgiveness: A True Story of Rape and Responsibility* and is co-authored by Thordis Elva and Tom Stranger.

DeShon's Story

The Burning Fiery Furnace

DeShon wrote to us, saying, "I started therapy recently and want to let you know how it's going. My dream log reveals a violent mental process, but I see improvement on the horizon." "Can you see my improvements and growing self-awareness in the following dreams?"

Dream #1
1 month into weekly therapy

"In the first dream, I was held down into a chair by four men who had kidnapped me and said they were the police even though it was obvious they were not real police. So the first guy was supposed to kick me, and he never did kick me, and so the boss man said I had to do five years in prison because that guy didn't kick me. Meanwhile, a third person was getting ready to break my arm while I was in the chair."

Meaning of the Dream: "Instead of being punished for wanting love and attention, perhaps a better way is to invoke self-love, self-care, and compassion for others."

Dream #2
2 months into weekly therapy

"While driving, I crashed into the back of a person's car, and for some reason, my vehicle kept going right over the top of his car, and I thought I had maybe crushed him. When I turned around to look, it was an ISIS member, so I kept going because I figured he wouldn't call the cops and risk being deported. Then I was worried about being caught by the police, and then my friends showed up, and they helped identify things on my vehicle that needed to be fixed. So, in addition to getting the car fixed, I also fixed my motorcycle and my bicycle because the wheels, tires, and different parts needed to be fixed up."

Meaning of the Dream: "The bottom line is that this dream made me look at my behavior towards others where I had been abusive, and I need to take ownership of that."

Dream #3
A few months into therapy

"I have had many recurring dreams from my teenage years into adulthood (current day) where I sneak up the laundry shoot to steal from my family or sneak into a roof access point to steal from a neighbor over and over again at the same neighbor's house, which makes me feel guilty, and I wonder why I've never been caught. In each dream, the path I am on is increasingly narrow."

"In other dreams, I flew above the people in a hotel or resort, such as those I used to party in, at the airport, or the grain

24

storage facility; in each place, I sought refuge, but the options became increasingly unviable and restricted."

"Tonight, however, I was not alone in my dream. I had a car full of older adults counting on me to drive my jeep through various rough terrains on a golf course, but the options kept getting narrower. I was quite the impressive driver, and the older adults were very calm and patient while I explored various options to get us all to where we were going."

Meaning of the Dream: "I am learning that Self-reliance is not an example of Servant Leadership."

Dream #4
A few more months into therapy

"I dreamt of being confronted by several large men in my parent's home gathered around the sink where they had something in a large, heavy container that was bloody, wet, and dripping onto the floor, missing a bucket they had placed there. I got mad and picked up the extremely heavy box, which fell to the floor.

"Nevertheless, I strengthened my back, lifted the box, carried it out of the kitchen, through the living room, to the front door, and threw it out onto the house's porch, letting it fall onto the first few steps. I

25

turned back into the living room and confronted one of the men as he raised his fist toward me; I raised my fist toward him. Then I woke up."

Meaning of the dream: "My goal is to find a better way to respond to the generational shame that shaped my family dynamics. Therapy is helping reshape my mental imagery and inventory."

Same Night: "The dream of confrontation was followed by a dream of being on the wrong freeway interchange, heading in the wrong direction."

"Upon awakening, I realized I must intentionally reach out to my life partner with goodwill, harmony, and forgiveness. We haven't spoken yet (in two years), but that's not bad while I reconcile my inner thoughts with Divine Awareness."

Dream #5
Several months into weekly therapy

"A woman (maybe my mom) killed a woman in her care by electrocution behind the refrigerator in her home. Mom and I then acted as if nothing had happened, but I was concerned that the murder would be exposed at some point, in particular, because the deceased woman's friends and family came to our home and asked about her and where her car was, that we had been driving."

"As a child, I knew something was wrong with our family dynamics, as did most of our neighbors. This dream means that I became a part of my parents' coverup even though I did not do the crime or know it had occurred, but I incurred and endured the shame."

Dream #6
Ready to pause therapy.

"I dreamt about urgently replacing Dad's gun and gloves in his drawer before he got home so he wouldn't know I had "been in there.""

"The meaning of this dream is that I spent my entire childhood hiding my activities and soul from "him" and became very good at it."

"I also dreamt about dozens and dozens of baby chickens. Later that day, while reading a long-lost friend's obituary, I discovered that he had enjoyed raising chickens when he was young."

Dream #7
Ready to stop therapy.

"I am trying to get through TSA while carrying illegal substances, and illegal thoughts are in my mind."

"Illegal thoughts: need to matter; need to care about others; positive self-appraisal; need to be a blessing to others; all of which are off-limits when you are in survival mode."

"I quit therapy to catch my breath, even
though the dreams were enlightening."

JJ's Story

Forgiving Pedophiles

JJ's story includes guidance from <u>Jocko Willink</u>, a retired U.S. Navy SEAL officer, co-author of the #1 New York Times bestseller Extreme Ownership: How U.S. Navy SEALs Lead and Win, Dichotomy of Leadership, host of the top-rated Jocko Podcast, and co-founder of Echelon Front, where he serves as Chief Executive Officer, leadership instructor, speaker, and strategic advisor. Jocko spent 20 years in the SEAL Teams, starting as an enlisted SEAL and rising to become a SEAL officer.

Jocko also authored the Discipline Equals Freedom Field Manual, a New York Times Bestseller, and the best-selling Way of the Warrior Kid children's book series.

JJ's Story from <u>Jocko's Podcast #184</u>: [Getting Over Abuse. Build Relationships as an Introvert] begins @ 1:42:55.

"Before JJ Doe was adopted, JJ was sexually abused for two years by a foster parent and others while living in their care. JJ grew up afraid of everything but eventually began playing sports and entered the army, where JJ felt completely unafraid of anything. When JJ exited the army, JJ got into a long-term relationship and told JJ's partner what had happened at the foster home, the first time JJ had told anyone what had happened. The partner encouraged JJ to reach out to the foster parents, and JJ did, which was a total disaster. The foster parents still had JJ's room, where all the bad stuff had happened, made up as if JJ had never left twenty years before when these horrors had occurred. JJ confronted the monster, who had done these things but failed to get a helpful or loving response. When confronted by JJ, the abuser responded with the same words spoken years ago while assaulting JJ, "Sometimes people change." Suddenly, JJ became a weak young person again and couldn't fight back. JJ left the foster parent's home with serious self-doubt. Ultimately, JJ became a respected cop and then a detective highly skilled at getting confessions from child rapists, murderers, and the like. JJ said, "It's terrible to hear what these animals do.

JJ's question to Jocko was, "Recently, the past has returned with a vengeance. I cannot get through a short time, maybe an hour, without thinking about my past and failure. The only time I have peace is when I destroy myself working out. I consider it as punishing myself and feel better when I do it. How can I stop this or at least manage it?

Jocko responded, "This is a horrible situation you had to live through as a kid or anyone; any human would have to go through this. As far as how you can manage this better, I will describe one of the blocks of training we go through in a SEAL platoon called close-quarters combat. You're in a thing called The Kill House with ballistic walls. There are targets in there, and you are moving around dynamically, shooting live-fire ammunition. People are six inches away from you while you're taking close shots. There is a lot of pressure in there. There are standard operating procedures and safety procedures that you have to follow. There is much processing, i.e., should I go left or right, is that a good guy or a bad guy, should I move or stay, how do I communicate that I need to move, should you shoot or not shoot at a target? And so, all these things are going on when you enter a room. All these things that you have to go through.

"All these steps you have to make and all these procedures you must follow. All these are decisions you have to make, and it all happens in a split second. And so, in a Kill House, the training cadres are above you on the catwalks, watching you closely. So, when a room entry happens, you get a lot of critique from the people on the catwalk. The cadre would say, "You could have done this, or you should have done that, or you could have moved left, or you should have pushed forward, or it would be better if you had done this other thing.

"At some point, I realized that all of the Kill House training is good, and I get it. Like, you have to get people to run the procedures correctly. But at a certain point, I wondered why we were doing this and getting all this negative feedback. The Kill House constructive feedback is similar to J's question about managing foster home abuse more healthily for a better outcome.

"Eventually, I would tell the SEAL team member, "Listen, you did what you did, and that's the decision you made at the time." And you know what? You could have done it in many different ways, but that's how you chose to do it, and that's okay. Now you have to move on. I don't like how you did it, and you don't like how you did it, but now we have to move on. You cannot take it back. What's done is done. The cadre doesn't like the way you did it. But that's okay.

"We don't get to rehearse these things until we do them perfectly because the Kill House will never be the same. Life and situations are constantly evolving and changing. We are not talking about rote memorization; we are in an active, changing, dangerous environment that requires instant decision-making. Maybe you acted too quickly or hesitated. Learning from what you did and trying to improve each time is the point.

"Instead of judging what you did, let's find out why you did what you did, i.e., why you made that decision. Now we have something on which we can improve. The question becomes, "What can I learn from this experience." "What can I take from this mistake and make me better?" "Maybe you were trying to protect yourself from more drama, and that was your instinct." We don't know what your other choices were or what the outcome of those decisions would have been. All we have to work with is, what we did at the time, and how we can learn about ourselves." Your choice feels like a bad decision, but you don't know what the outcome of the other decisions would have been.

"You cannot change the outcome of what happened in the past. You cannot do it. But what you can do is you can grow from it. You can learn from it. You can take that scenario and mentally replay it in your head and figure out if there would have been or could have been a better outcome. Or maybe your outcome wasn't that bad or as bad as some other outcome. But that is where you are right now. You can't change the outcome of something that has occurred in the past.

A dichotomy story from Jocko: "While you cannot change the past, you can change how you perceive the past. As an example, if someone gets fired from their job. Their confidence goes down, they get depressed, and they decide not to apply for a new job because they "don't deserve a good job." Eventually, they apply for a lesser job and, who knows, maybe start drinking to relieve their depression, and now they are late; they end up on a downward spiral. We would look at them being fired as something that destroyed their life. That's how we would perceive it. They were fine until they got fired, lost their confidence, and are now in a bad place.

"But, if that person got fired from their job, and instead it was a wake-up call for them to apply for a better job. Maybe they got rejected from many applications, but they are on a different trajectory; Maybe they took a lesser-paying job and realized a mistake was made at the prior job and began "getting after it" at the new job, and then they got promoted; and then they got promoted again because they were fully committed to working harder and being better at what they were doing. And eventually, maybe they took over the whole company. And this isn't a crazy idea; this isn't too far-fetched; this can happen and does happen all the time. But in this scenario, we would perceive the firing as the catalyst that improved their life. And there are all kinds of examples like that in the world.

"The past cannot be changed. But the past can change you for the better, or it can change you for the worse. My question is, "Why not make it for the better?" We hear the term narrative used often in the political arena. Your mental narrative supports the overarching goal or value about what happened in your past. You get to write the narrative. It's not a fabrication, but you get to write the reality of where you end up. You get to write it. You get to control your mental narrative. So, what I am saying is, take control of that narrative. That horrible story in your past ends the way you want. You control that narrative. You control that story, so make that story good. Make that story epic. Make the direction of your life heroic.

"And that's how I think you can take control or handle better the horrible stuff you went through." ~ *Jocko*

John's Story

Forgiving Sexual Assault

When Pastor John Gray was four years old, two boys held him down on the front lawn of his parent's home and sexually assaulted him in broad daylight. John lived with this traumatic event and told no one until he was 19.

John's secret shame was made worse when he told his mother he had a wet dream at puberty, to which she scolded him, "Go pray to the Lord and ask for forgiveness and take a bath."

You can listen to Pastor John's story in his compelling interview with Cam Newton, NFL Quarterback, titled "Overcoming Childhood Molestation: Pastor John Gray" - on Funky Friday Podcast.

Part II

Unconscious Patterns

"You don't blame people for having unconscious patterns. You try to make them conscious of it. Becoming conscious allows a person to become response-able (two words).

"Our personalities are a defense mechanism on a survival/optimization continuum. Pain reduction is programmed into our brains, i.e., a childhood survival adaptation response.

"Addiction is any behavior in that a person finds temporary pleasure or relief and therefore craves but suffers negative consequences in the long-term and cannot give it up, e.g., sex, gambling, shopping, eating, work, exercise, internet, gaming, pornography, investing, political power, or the acquisition of wealth.

"Addiction is our attempt to regulate an unbearable emotional state through external means." ~ *Dr. Gabor Maté*

Click here or search YouTube for – "Your Personality Is a Defensive Cover" ~ *Dr. Gabor Maté*

Baths of Mindfulness

So, how do we become aware of our unconscious patterns? You guessed it, we pray and meditate on our relationship with Divine Awareness.

Thich Nhat Hanh, a Buddhist monk, a Nobel Peace Prize nominee, and an international speaker, refers to our unconscious patterns as seeds. In his book titled, "Reconciliation: Healing the Inner Child," Thich says:

"Mental formations like anger, sorrow, or joy rest in the sub-consciousness as seeds. We have a seed of anger, despair, discrimination, fear, a seed of mindfulness, compassion, a seed of understanding.

"Our subconscious is made of the totality of the seeds, and the soil preserves and maintains all the seeds.

"The seeds stay there until we hear, see, read, or think of something that touches a seed. It makes us feel anger, joy, or sorrow, a seed coming up and manifesting on a level of everyday consciousness.

"For example, whenever a seed of anger comes into our everyday consciousness, we can touch the seed of mindfulness and invite it to come up simultaneously.

"Every time we need the energy of mindfulness, we touch that seed with our mindful breathing, mindful walking, smiling, and then we have the energy ready to do the work of recognizing, embracing, and later on looking deeply and transforming life experiences.

"Our seeds of pain, sorrow, anger, and despair always want to come to our daily consciousness because they've grown big and need our attention. They want to emerge, but we don't want these uninvited guests to come up because they are painful to experience. So we tried to block their way. We want them to stay asleep. We don't want to face them, so our habit fills our minds with other guests.

"Whenever we have 10 or 15 minutes of free time, we do anything we can to stay occupied. We call a friend, pick up a book, turn on the television, or go for a drive. We hope these unpleasant mental formations will not arise if our mind is occupied.

"But all mental formations need to circulate if we don't let them come up. Otherwise, we have bad circulation in our psyche, and symptoms of mental illness and depression begin to manifest in our minds and body.

"Every time you give your subconscious thoughts a bath of mindfulness, your pain blocks become lighter. So give your anger, despair, and fear a bath of mindfulness daily.

"After several days or weeks of bringing them up and helping them back down again, you create good circulation in your psyche." ~ *Thich Nhat Hanh*

Adversity Responses

Dear Ego-self, I see you are responding to trauma in the only way you know how. ~ Selah

While unskilled and unlearned, we respond to adversity in ways that come from our reptilian brain, i.e., greed, lust, envy, showing up as lying, cheating, and stealing. Once we overcome adversity or it dies off naturally, we sometimes continue with these survival tools without thinking about them, and they show up as character defects. Character defects are any unnecessary survival tool that causes harm to our relationship with ourselves and others.

Counseling and 12-Step programs may be necessary for a person to realize that external adversity has ceased and we only perceive adversity, albeit in our mind, as not happening to us any longer.

Adversity or Compassion

Compassion, understanding, patience, and humility are the character traits we seek in our relationship with Divine Awareness. If we experience troubled thinking, we purposefully take time out to focus on our Ego-selves and ask, "What does my Ego-self want" "What does my Ego-self need," and "How can I please my Ego-self without damaging myself and others?"

Embracing our thoughts and feelings mindfully, we realize that our Ego-selves desire compassion, understanding, patience, and humility, but we have relied on getting those things from someone else. In today's world, that "someone else" often fails to provide the compassion, hope, patience, and understanding we demand from them, which leaves a void in us.

So how do we get the compassion, understanding, and patience we need to fill that void? First, we have to understand what "it" is we are looking for, what "it" tastes like, and what "it" feels like.

Compassion, understanding, patience, and humility are the actions, words, and thoughts we use to communicate with ourselves and others when we act with self-care. Our relationship with Divine Awareness protects us from bullies and helps us overcome obstacles.

Garden of Memories

Mentally, we are in the Garden of Eden, alone or with a group. Our mind is a Garden of Memories, knowing and experiencing good and evil. Mindfully, we strive to experience Divine Awareness in our Gardens of Eden and Memories.

Like the biblical Garden of Eden, our body and mind, or "Gardens of Memories," become the Tree of Life and knowledge of Good and Evil.

The Divine Awareness of God does not dwell "somewhere out there" beyond our reach. Rather, within each person is the knowledge of a power greater than ourselves.

Embracing Divine Awareness, we intuitively know how to handle situations that used to baffle us and the difference between good and evil.

Was it good or evil to punish Adam and Eve for their curiosity?

Ego-Self's Craving

Above all else, our Ego-self, a.k.a. inner child, seeks attention upon itself. Our Ego-self causes us to crave attention at our core. We all do this. Some of us enjoy plenty of positive and constructive attention from others, helping us grow and flourish throughout our lives.

Some of us seek attention by associating with those we know to suffer. We associate with criminals or drug addicts because they won't challenge or deny our suffering. They will agree with our suffering as if to say, "Yes, I, too, am suffering," and "My self-destructive behavior proves to you that we are the same, and we both suffer."

Positive attention assuages our instinctual desire to be fed, to be clothed, and to be sheltered. We behave "properly" to assure ourselves of food, safety, and shelter, whether at work or home. We behave badly occasionally, but we know the limits of how far to go in our bad behavior before encountering dangerous consequences.

Sometimes, though, we learn of a consequence after it is too late to correct our bad behavior, causing us to lose access to food, safety, and shelter.

We become divorced because of our selfish acts. Our family and friends disown us because of our fear-based behavior, which causes pain to them and causes pain to ourselves.

Lacking enough positive, healthy interaction and attention to our relationship with Divine Awareness, our Ego-self engulfs us with worry and tension. We become frustrated and afraid. We do not admit to others that we are afraid, but we are.

We might be consciously unaware of our fear, but we are afraid even so. In this state of fear, we lash out at those whom we perceive to be denying us access to food, denying our access to shelter, and denying our access to safety.

We self-destruct with alcohol, drugs, excessive shopping, repetitive harmful physical activity, and worrisome thoughts because we suffer.

When we suffer, we bully others. We bully ourselves. We may suffer so much that we seek to kill ourselves or others to "tell others" of our suffering. Some of us believe that killing others and ourselves is the only solution we dare to imagine. We say, "I will get much attention if I do this," and, "I will no longer suffer."

The negative impact of bullying is profound and may be long-lasting. Not only will the bully cause physical harm to themselves and others, but our fear-based response to the bully also creates energy blockages in our body, our mind, and energy blockages in our soul.

Long after the bully is gone, we may feel helpless and ashamed of being abused by the bully. Some of us will take our own lives due to bullying unless we find a relationship with Divine Awareness.

Ego-Self vs. Bullies

If we suffered at the hands of a bully, we might again become frozen at the mere memory of those event(s). Today, perceiving a similar situation, our Ego-self returns to a fight, flight or freeze mode, reliving hopelessness, fear, and shame. We experience the same feelings that arose when one of life's bullies (or our self-bullying) threatened and harassed us during an earlier time.

We might realize that our Ego-self is currently in a fear state, but until now, we had no idea how to resolve the issue. We blamed others and ourselves, which did nothing to resolve our dilemma because we failed to include Divine Awareness in our solution.

Family, friends, and coworkers perceive our unhappiness and fear state, but they are also unskilled in helping resolve our dilemmas. They observe us like an animal at the zoo, saying, "Gosh, what a curious and unfortunate predicament you are in."

But they do little or nothing to help because they, too, are frozen in selfishness and material consumption, unaware of any solution to our Ego-self's dilemma. They are unaware that Divine Awareness solves our dilemma.

That is not to say our lives are hopeless; certain parts may need repair. Before embracing our life of self-care, we experienced unsettledness when thinking about personal safety, personal relations, sexual relations, or financial and material well-being.

Dialoguing with a priest, a therapist, a counselor, or a psychiatrist allows us to share our blocked energy and set ourselves free.

Speaking with trusted friends accomplishes a similar outcome assuming we are willing to bare our souls to them. Baring our souls releases us from a prison of doom, gloom, and fear. Baring our souls allows us to perceive fresh new options and new choices.

Our Ego-self involves itself in our body, mind, and soul, whether we want it to do so or not. Our Ego-self stands guard over its territory, protecting us with great force whether we ask it to do so or not. Our Ego-self is the barking dog that protects its owner relentlessly.

We aim to comfort our Ego-self and let it know that we appreciate its hard work. Like the canines protecting us throughout history, our Ego-selves demand recognition and approval for their hard work. Our Ego-self deserves our respect and admiration.

Ego-Self or Satan

Our Ego-self is an untamed force within us that demands unequivocal fairness and "maybe a little extra if we can rise above the others." Satan is the kinetic, outward, and tangible expression of a person's or group's lust, envy, anger, and desire for revenge. When someone or a group of people acts badly, violently, or with evil intent, we say that they are filled with the devil or possessed by Satan, which is entirely accurate.

When the bible talks about Satan being expelled from heaven, or "the Fall of Mankind, " they describe our innate behaviors of envy, lust, fear, and shame, i.e., "we are not being treated fairly, so we must "do a little more and get creative" to even the score and perhaps rise above the threat. Satan is not "out there somewhere." It is the bad behavior within us and our response to perceived threats and opportunities.

Our Ego-self is the emotional brain within us, our *Satan in the Garden of Eden*, perceiving threats and opportunities here and now based on past experiences, whether the current mental image is a memory or a future event.

51

Without our daily reliance on Divine Awareness, our Ego-selves replay each past, present, and future emotional event until we receive an answer that calms our fear and unsettledness. We suffer until we come up with the right answer for our Ego-selves. We suffer because we failed to include Divine Awareness in our proposed solution to our problems. We failed to give our Ego-selves a suitable answer, a workable solution to our dilemma that includes Divine Awareness.

When we look only to ourselves for the answer to our suffering, we find no real solution and believe that none exists. Assuming no solution exists, we find alcohol, addictions, and other deadly behaviors as substitutes. If our suffering is great enough, we call on a higher power to help out momentarily until our fear subsides. In the meantime, we muddle along, wondering when and how our suffering will end. We wonder when our emptiness will be replaced with a feeling of wholeness and well-being toward others.

Finding our resolve, we try again to rely on Divine Awareness to resolve our suffering and the suffering of others.

Our Emptiness

Without Divine Awareness, our Ego-selves often feel empty. Emptiness happens when we refuse to speak the language of Divine Awareness, kindness, and encouragement to ourselves and others. Emptiness is the price for using defeatist, blaming language instead of empowering thoughts and actions.

Throughout time, prophets and spirit-guides spoke of how to embrace and replace the emptiness within us. These people (think of Mother Teresa, Jesus, Muhammad, and Buddha) told us to embrace Divine Awareness with compassion, understanding, patience, humility, and forgiveness toward ourselves and others.

Without knowing better, we thought that compassion, understanding, patience, and humility were things to be **received** before they were given to someone else. Selfish to our core, we said, "Why should I give something away when I have received so little of it," or "How can I give away something that I don't have?"

Giving compassion, understanding, and humility fills the void within us. Giving another person words of kindness and encouragement creates a feeling of wholeness and purpose. Giving words of kindness and encouragement instills a sense of prosperity in those who receive them and those who give them away.

The purpose of this book is to invite our Ego-selves into a relationship with Divine Awareness so that we begin to understand how giving something away benefits us as much or more than the other person.

How do we transform our "me—me—me" consumption-based thinking and turn it outward? We learn the language of the heart and apply it to our daily thoughts, words, prayers, and actions by embracing our life of self-care.

Talking with our Ego-selves in an enlightened manner requires using an intuitive language, the Language of the Heart. Using a language that includes words such as *compassion, understanding, patience,* and *humility* is comforting to our Ego-selves and an expression of mindfulness and wellness in our lives.

So, what keeps us from empowering ourselves with gifts of compassion and understanding, let alone giving those gifts to our family, friends, and passersby?

We often run away or neglect our obligations and duties instead of protecting ourselves with gifts of kindness and encouragement. We run from our thoughts, our unsettledness. We blame others; We create, hoard, cling to the past, and grasp material solutions and more time. All the while, our Ego-selves wait, feeling empty until we return to our relationship with Divine Awareness.

Divine Awareness watches us scurrying back and forth in a panic as we attempt to manage our lives, masking the suffering of our Ego-selves as if everything is okay. Without knowing better, we refuse to try the actions of Divine Awareness until our suffering becomes unbearable.

Our Ego-self's demand for attention is unrelenting, so the best thing to do is respond to our Ego-self and ask, "What can I do for you today?" For example, we might say:

"Ego-self, would you like to stop by and say hello?"

"Ego-self, is this a good time to talk?"

"Ego-self, I would like to make amends for how I treated you recently."

"Yes, dear Ego-self, you felt an injustice done to you; let's pray for someone else's injustice so that we both experience healing."

Unless we embrace the gifts of Divine Awareness, our Ego-selves remain unsettled by life's obstacles. We fail our Ego-selves when we exclude the gifts of Divine Awareness from our plans.

We make amends to our Ego-selves by speaking from our heart, saying:

"Ego-self, I understand where you seek to be understood."

"Ego-self, I offer compassion to you where you have suffered."

"Ego-self, I offer harmony where you are in discord."

"Ego-self, I offer patience where you are unsettled and afraid."

"Ego-self, I offer forgiveness, where you have no debt to pay."

We look within ourselves for our relationship with Divine Awareness, the willingness and the ability to speak these words from our hearts meaningfully.

It is wise to know what the Ego-self is to prevent our Ego-self from hijacking our emotions. Our Ego-self, after all, is the permanent resident in our Gardens of Eden, our Garden of Memories and Expectations (our minds and our inner selves). Our Ego-self is the gatekeeper of our dignity and peaceful relationships.

Knowing our Ego-selves begins with introspection and asking, "What keeps me from embracing and enjoying my life of Divine Awareness each day?" and "What does my

Ego-self need from me as I renew my relationship with Divine Awareness?"

Our Ego-self needs assurance that we have a sustainable relationship with Divine Awareness. Our Ego-self will not trust us without Divine Awareness on the team.

We cannot say to someone else, "Dear loved one, will you comfort my Ego-self for me while I attend to material things, my kids, my job?" No, we must take part with our hands, feet, eyes, and mouth in comforting our Ego-selves. We aim to comfort our Ego-selves by entering into our relationship with Divine Awareness and acting toward others with understanding and compassion.

Whether the Ego-self is ours or someone else's, we rely on Divine Awareness to help us attend to all Ego-selves. Our purpose in life is to fill the void in ourselves and each other so that we experience wholeness and well-being.

We do not need to receive anything externally to fill the void. We look to Divine Awareness to show us the way to our well-being and the well-being of our friends and family.

We begin our conversation with our Ego-self by asking ourselves questions:

"When I need companionship, what do my Ego-self and Divine Awareness say about this plan?"

"Are my Ego-self and the gifts of Divine Awareness fully incorporated into my plan?"

Or does my Ego-self say, "Companionship did not work out in the past; it's better to stay alone in a state of fear." Our Ego-selves "drive the bus," so to speak, so we had better pay attention to the direction our Ego-self is going. Our Ego-selves select from yes-or-no choices such as the following:

"Yes, I like companionship," or "No, I don't like companionship."

"Yes, I like risk-taking," or "No, I don't."

"Yes, I like exploring," or "No, I don't like exploring."

We must observe our Ego-self and consider whether it is acting in our best interest.

Without Divine Awareness guidance in the form of thoughts, words, and deeds of compassion, understanding, patience, and humility, our Ego-selves spin out of control.

Hijacked Ego

To avoid being hijacked by our negative self-talk, our Ego-self requires gifts of compassion, understanding, patience, and humility. Without such gifts and attention, our Ego-self provokes us, and it bullies everyone around us because it feels empty and alone.

We communicate with our Ego-self through prayer and meditation. We start this communication by welcoming and embracing Divine Awareness. Our Ego-self is waiting for us to show up in a relationship with Divine Awareness, not to show up with the same hopeless answer of blaming others and ourselves for our suffering.

Meditation and prayer take courage, strength, and focus. We need the courage to invite our Ego-selves to converse with us. In meditation, we look to Divine Awareness for the words and strength to comfort our Ego-self when it speaks the truth. We focus on our goal of bringing gifts of compassion and neutrality to our Ego-self, which is a life purpose. We also bring gifts of encouragement when we express gratitude, trust, and humility toward ourselves and others.

Empowered by our relationship with Divine Awareness, we bring our Ego-selves' gifts of compassion, understanding, patience, and humility. As a result of our gift-giving, we feel peace and happiness right now. We create this process several times daily because of our Ego-self's desire and demand for the constant flow of God's Divine energy.

During conversations with our Ego-self, our body, mind, and spirit will confirm that the Ego-self exists within us. We might experience goosebumps or a nervous twitch as our Ego-self settles in for the conversation. Our Ego-self may cause us to weep or cry as it unveils secret memories and thoughts.

Our Ego-self welcomes spiritual gifts from us, but giving others our Divine Awareness feels even better. Our Ego-self feels fulfilled when we give Divine Awareness gifts to someone else. This is the connection in life. Giving our compassion to someone else benefits all of us.

When hijacked by fear, we withhold the empowering gifts of understanding, compassion, patience, and humility as if they do not exist or cannot be replaced.

Luckily, we have a solution to transform ourselves away from hoarding gifts; by following the Divine Awareness examples mentioned throughout this book and other sources.

Part III

Why Meditate?

Taking a bath of mindfulness or "cleaning up our side of the street," as we say in the 12-Step programs, includes cleaning up our conscious and subconscious thoughts. So, how do we do this? We practice prayer and meditation daily.

During meditation, we look into our subconscious thoughts and converse with our inner child and Ego-self. We enter the Burning Fiery Furnace of our soul, our innermost thoughts, with our labels and self-doubt to emerge unharmed from the self-analysis. ~ *Daniel 3:1*

Meditation allows us to quietly welcome and contemplate our Ego-self, negative self-talk, and self-strengths and consider them with kindness and compassion and without judgment.

"When I first approached my inner child, it screamed, "Get the hell out of here and never come back" as it retreated to a corner of the room. So, I left, returned a few days later, and just sat with the child, not saying a word, just breathing in and out." ~ *Selah*

Meditation – What is It?

Meditation is to quietly welcome and contemplate our Ego-self, negative self-talk, and self-strengths and consider them with kindness and compassion.

Our Ego-self is always on guard, always vigilant, and always protecting us from real or imagined bullies.

Whether the bully exists here or now, our Ego-self responds to everything it perceives as true. The protective nature of our Ego-self requires that we treat it with Divine Awareness to have something to offer others. This takes daily practice as the Ego-self wakes up each morning.

Our purpose, then, is to search our Ego-self and to soothe it with our peaceful mind. We call on Divine Awareness to envelop our mind, body, and soul with peaceful thoughts, lest we become hijacked by our Ego-self's fear and selfishness.

Meditation is the process of caretaking our Ego-self and seeking guidance from Divine Awareness. Meditation is a process of intentional thinking, engaging our imagination for a specific purpose, such as overcoming life's obstacles and negative self-talk.

Meditation is a process of claiming a new reality for us — a new, stronger, healthier perception of ourselves — a stronger, healthier way to engage with others. Meditation is the pathway to a healthy relationship with Divine Awareness.

We gently pray about compassion, understanding, patience, forgiveness, or gratitude during meditation.

Speaking our prayer out loud may inspire us to write our prayer on paper to refer to later when we need inspiration or to share our meditation with a trusted friend.

During meditation, we focus on sending compassion, understanding, or gratitude to a person, place, or situation.

Imagining ourselves as a third person is a starting point. During meditation, we call ourselves by our name or by another name; we realize the difference between a person doing the meditation and the person for whom we are praying and meditating.

To meditate, we sit on a pad on the floor in a quiet space with our backs supported against a bed or sofa so that we don't slouch. We place our hands on our knees, our palms facing upward, closing our thumbs and first fingers. Coffee or tea are great companions. We turn off or silence our cell phones. We let others know we are meditating, and they will leave us in peace for a time.

We sit for ten or twenty minutes, activating our intentional mind. We expect an awareness of God's Divine knowledge and revelation.

We breathe in. We breathe out.

Yes, there is a benefit to making a gentle *om* ("Om," "Aum") sound at the beginning of our meditation and during our meditation. We make this gentle sound to notify our body and mind that we are meditating. We tell our bodies, "I am okay; you are okay." We are telling our minds, "I am okay; you are okay."

We gently push our lower jawbone slightly forward and say *"om"* toward the back of our throat, causing the sound to resonate throughout our sinuses. We *om* as if we are calming a baby with our deep, strong, soothing sound. Our mouths are closed, and we use a downward voice. We inhale through our nose slowly and fully until we cannot breathe more air and hold it momentarily as we smile a half-smile. We exhale slowly and completely through our nose with our mouth closed until the entire depth of our lungs exhale and hold as we smile a half-smile.

After a few breaths to calm our mind, to calm our body, we focus on the energy of our body, the energy of our mind. We connect with our Ego-self as if embarking on a voyage, an adventure, a journey.

We are alert and awake. We are calm. We are at peace. We are alive. We are present right here, right now.

During meditation, we slow down our breathing. We slow down our minds. We listen to our body to find out where our body is tense and where our body stores anxiety. Our body might twitch as tension is released. We welcome this saying, "Dear body, you are speaking to me. Thank you. I am listening to you."

When our brain sends a thought or many thoughts to us, we welcome our thoughts by saying, "Dear lovely brain, you are communicating with me." We focus only on the thought on which we intend to focus. We let the other thoughts pass by, like leaves floating away from us on the river.

We listen to our bodies and observe our thoughts as we breathe quietly and calmly with a half-smile. During each meditation, we speak with our Ego-self like a loved one, with someone who needs our compassion, understanding, patience, and protection.

Meditation aims to get to know ourselves and our Ego-self so that we are okay with being known to others. We become our authentic selves, and we make no apologies for our behavior; we make no apologies for our thinking.

Through daily practice, we learn to meditate while walking. We learn to meditate while standing in an elevator. We learn to meditate during a break from a conversation with a colleague, friend, or coworker.

We create a single meditation once daily and repeat it throughout the day for the best results.

Benefits of Meditation

Before knowing and relying on Divine Awareness, we spoke to ourselves in defeatist, blaming language. We ran scared of the images produced onto the screens of our minds by the Ego-self.

In meditation, we comfort ourselves by acknowledging our concerns and nervousness by speaking words of Divine Awareness, kindness, and encouragement daily. We produce calming thoughts and pleasant scenarios as if we are already calm and collected, comforting a newborn baby. We fake it until we make it, if necessary.

Our Ego-self fights back, saying to us, "But what about this bad person or that horrible situation" or "If only he would act this way," or "If only they would not do what they are doing," or "But I am unsettled."

Our Ego-self will only stop once we respond appropriately to each unsettled thought in our mind with an answer which includes Divine Awareness as our primary solution.

Meditations on Others

We experience joy by doing something for someone else. We listen to a dear friend and spend time with a loved one.

We recall the most peaceful moment in our lives, the most wonderful moment, and then we pray for that moment to occur in someone else's life.

We become willing to donate our uplifting moment to someone who is suffering.

During our meditation, we send Divine Awareness, joy, and success to those we know and have never met.

If we desire financial well-being for ourselves, we pray for someone else to achieve financial well-being so that the energy of financial well-being is "in the air."

If we desire a loving spouse, we pray for someone else to find their soulmate so that "trust-filled love is in the air."

If we are ill, we pray for our friend's health and well-being so that "good health and well-being abound in them and us."

If we suffer from addiction, we pray for someone else to recover from their addiction so that sobriety comes to them and us.

Praying for others affirms our wholeness and brings Divine Awareness to the other person and us.

Meditations on Anxiety

During our daily practice of self-awareness, we create our prayers or rely on other prayers and meditations. We pray the prayers for ourselves, and we pray for someone else.

In the following meditations, we speak the language of Divine Awareness, kindness, and encouragement and begin to express ourselves with those qualities in our daily lives.

We create only one meditation per day, lest we overindulge.

Anxiety: Meditation 1
Dear Anxiety, you have arrived, seeking comfort and safe boundaries from life's bullies. ~ *Divine Awareness*

> I breathe in Divine Awareness to share the gifts of safe boundaries for myself and others.

> Breathing out, I let anxiety float away like a leaf on the river.

Anxiety: Meditation 2

Dear Anxiety, you exist wherever I perceive one of life's bullies. Would you like to talk? ~ *Selah*

I breathe in Divine Awareness to share the empowering gifts of compassion toward myself and others.

Breathing out, I let anxiety float away from me like a leaf going by on the river.

Anxiety: Meditation 3

Dear Anxiety and Fear, I offer forgiveness where you cannot pay your debt. ~ *Selah*

I breathe in Divine Awareness to share the gifts of forgiveness for myself and others.

Breathing out, I let anxiety and fear float away from me like leaves going by on the river.

Anxiety: Meditation 4

Dear Anxiety, the bully has long since departed. Are you willing to embrace the patience and humility I gave you? ~ *Divine Awareness*

Receiving the gifts of patience and humility, I breathe in.

72

Breathing out, I let anxiety float
away like a leaf on the river.

Anxiety: Meditation 5
Dear Anxiety and Fear, I see you are
restless and discontent from dealing
with life's bullies of shame and
remorse. Would you like to talk now? ~
Divine Awareness

I breathe in Divine Awareness to
share the empowering gifts of
compassion toward myself and
others.

Breathing out, I let troubling
thoughts float away like leaves
on the river.

Anxiety: Meditation 6
Dear Anxiety and Fear, I am here to
understand where you seek to be
understood. ~ *Selah*

I breathe in Divine Awareness to
share the empowering gifts of
understanding with others.

Breathing out, I let troubling
thoughts float away like leaves
on the river.

Anxiety: Meditation 7
Dear thieves named anxiety and fear, I
offer compassion where you have
caused suffering to others. ~ *Selah*

73

I breathe in Divine Awareness to share the empowering gifts of compassion toward myself and others.

Breathing out, I let troubling thoughts float away like leaves on the river.

Anxiety: *Meditation 8*

Dear Anxiety and Fear, I offer harmony where you feel nervousness. ~ *Selah*

I breathe in Divine Awareness to share the gifts of harmony with others.

Breathing out, I let nervousness float away like a leaf on the river.

Anxiety: *Meditation 9*

Dear Anxiety and Fear, the loving character trait of patience is within me. ~ *Selah*

I breathe in Divine Awareness to share the empowering gifts of patience with myself and others.

Breathing out, I let anxiety and fear float away from me like leaves on the river.

Meditations on Negative Self-Talk

Reflecting on my wounds at the hands of life's bullies, I asked my Ego-self, "Why are you tattered and in disarray?" "Who did that to you?" "I will get even with everyone who mistreated you." —Responding to me, my Ego-self said, "Look in the mirror, my beloved. You have done this to me."

To soothe our Ego-self, we search ourselves to find the deepest, darkest secrets in us, which is no easy task. A journey of this magnitude takes meditation, prayer (lots of it), preparation (coffee and tea), and daily dedication.

Meditation is an opportunity to explore our mind, an opportunity to explore our body, and an opportunity to explore our thoughts. When a thought crosses our mind during meditation, we become aware of our neuro-biological reaction to the thought. We become aware of our bodies and aware of our emotions. We notice whether we are happy, sad, or anxious about the thought.

We observe each thought as if we are approaching a small child who needs our help. We say, "Dear thought, may I sit with you?" Or we may say, "Dear thought, may I talk with you," or "Dear thought, from where did you come? Please join me in conversation so that we will know each other."

Perhaps our thought is suffering, at which point we say to our thought:

"Dear thought, I understand where you seek understanding,"

"Dear thought, I offer compassion where you suffer."

"Dear thought, I offer patience where you are unsettled and impatient."

"Dear thought, I forgive you."

Perhaps our thought is very persistent in seeking our attention the way a small child demands it when they have something important to say.

Perhaps one of life's bullies is seeking our attention. The reason for this persistent thought is that we have spent countless hours denying this thought. We ran from this thought, hoping it would go away. We drank, and we drugged at this thought.

In meditation, we realize this thought needs compassion, understanding, patience, and humility.

"Dear persistent, troublesome thought, you are still with me. Come closer so that I will know you and understand you." ~ *Selah*

When we struggle with a persistent thought, we imagine other people who may be struggling with this same thought. Many of us struggle with the same thoughts as several billion people. The loving and powerful way to overcome our thoughts is to pray for someone else's worrisome thoughts.

When we pray for someone else and meditate on their well-being, we imagine that person overcoming a troublesome thought. As we meditate on someone else's well-being and Divine Awareness, we perceive a sense of well-being within ourselves. We perceive a sense of wholeness in ourselves. We are fulfilled, grateful, calm, and powerful.

We create or rely on other prayers and meditations during our daily Divine Awareness and self-reflection practice. We pray the prayer for ourselves, and we pray our prayer for someone else.

In the following meditations, we speak the language of Divine Awareness, kindness, and encouragement and begin to express ourselves with those qualities in our daily lives.

We create only one meditation per day, lest we overindulge.

Negative Self-talk: Meditation 1
Dear negative self-talk, may I sit with you? ~ *Selah*

Aware of the empowering gifts of self-awareness, I breathe in.

Breathing out, I embrace inspired thinking, Divine Awareness.

Negative Self-talk: Meditation 2
Dear Ego-self, it would help if you had a safe harbor. Welcome to our conversation. I want to know you better. ~ *Selah*

I breathe in Divine Awareness to share a trusted friend's desire to communicate with me.

Breathing out, I protect others with my inspired thinking, Divine Awareness.

Negative Self-talk: Meditation 3
Dear hijacked emotional thoughts. I offer compassion wherever you exist. ~ *Selah*

I breathe in Divine Awareness to share the gifts of compassion toward myself and others.

78

Breathing out, I embrace inspired thinking, Divine Awareness.

Negative Self-talk: Meditation 4

Dear hijacked emotional thoughts. I understand where you seek to be understood. I offer harmony and forgiveness to you. ~ *Selah*

I breathe in Divine Awareness to share the empowering gifts of harmony with myself and others.

I let emotional thoughts float away from me like leaves on a river.

Negative Self-talk: Meditation 5

Divine Awareness, I have bullied others when I felt frustrated. ~ *Selah*

I breathe in Divine Awareness to share the empowering gifts of forgiveness toward myself and others.

Breathing out, I let frustration float away like a leaf on the river.

Negative Self-talk: Meditation 6

Dear Ego-self, your suffering arrived when you planned for revenge. Thank you for sharing your truth with me. ~ *Selah*

I breathe in Divine Awareness to share the empowering gifts of honesty with myself and others.

Breathing out, I let revenge float away from me like a leaf on the river.

Negative Self-talk: Meditation 7

Dear Ego-self, your fear has no beginning and no end. How should I respond to you? ~ Selah

I breathe in Divine Awareness to share the empowering gifts of understanding with others.

Breathing out, I let character weaknesses float away like leaves on the river.

Negative Self-talk: Meditation 8

Dear Unsettledness, you have no beginning and no end. How should I respond to you? ~ Selah

Aware of the gifts of self-awareness, I breathe in.

Breathing out, I let unsettledness float away like a leaf on the river.

Negative Self-talk: Meditation 9

Dear Ego-self, in the form of my skin and bones, your secret thoughts create distance between Divine Awareness and me. ~ Selah

I breathe in Divine Awareness to
share the gifts of sharing with a
trusted friend.

Breathing out, I protect others
with my inspired thinking, Divine
Awareness.

Negative Self-talk: Meditation 10

Dear Ego-self, you are fraught with
anxiety over when and to whom you
will disclose your character
weaknesses. May we talk now? ~ *Divine
Awareness*

I breathe in Divine Awareness to
share the gifts of openness and
honesty toward myself and
others.

Breathing out, I embrace inspired
thinking, Divine Awareness.

Negative Self-talk: Meditation 11

Dear Ego-self, truth-telling gives you
hope and peace. ~ *Selah*

I breathe in the Divine Awareness
of honesty toward myself and
others.

Breathing out, I protect others
with my inspired thinking, Divine
Awareness.

Negative Self-talk: Meditation 12

Dear Ego-self, you have spoken the truth to me. Please, continue our conversation. ~ Selah

Breathing in, I know new energy flows through my body and mind.

Breathing out, I embrace inspired thinking, Divine Awareness.

Meditations on Revenge

Empowered with Divine Awareness, we stop thinking about revenge. We stop planning for revenge.

During our life of self-reliance and fear-driven thinking, when life's bullies attacked, we planned for revenge. We thought of revenge once or twice, or we thought of revenge all day, every day. We became unable to stop our thoughts of revenge.

Instead of seeking revenge, consider the story of Tammy, who let go of her desire for revenge and overcame a bully:

> "Plotting for revenge poisoned my heart and never resulted in its desired outcome. Hoping someone would die or promising, "I will kill that so and so," usually meant I would start at the bar with several rounds of alcohol "to get ready for the act of revenge." But, in reality, the night would be gone, nobody got hurt, and I woke up ruing the day I was born with a nightmarish hangover. I would do this over and over again."

"During meditation, I suffered while looking into my desire for revenge. I found my suffering. I found the suffering of Humanity. I found the suffering of one of life's bullies who behaved badly toward me."

"During meditation, I invited revenge to sit with me. I invited revenge to disclose its nature to me, to disclose itself to my body and mind. As revenge revealed itself to me, I experienced compassion. I understood where revenge sought to explain itself. I felt patience where revenge had suffered and humility for its truth. Compassion for revenge began to flow from me."

"During meditation, revenge transformed itself. My body tension diminished. Peacefulness and gratitude returned to my body and returned to my mind. Meditating on revenge allowed it to express itself. Meditation created an awareness of inspired and peaceful thoughts."

Empowered with Divine Awareness, we pray for others who suffered from thoughts of revenge at some time in their lives. We imagine a person we can pray for so their healing process will begin.

In the following meditations, we speak the language of kindness and encouragement and begin to express ourselves with those qualities in our daily lives.

We create only one meditation per day, lest we overindulge.

Revenge: Meditation 1
Dear Revenge, you arrived battered and bruised in defeat. Welcome; let me comfort you. ~ *Selah*

> I breathe in Divine Awareness to share the empowering gifts of compassion toward myself and others.

> Breathing out, I protect others with my inspired thinking, Divine Awareness.

Revenge: Meditation 2
Dear Revenge, your self-pleasuring has no limit in its depravity. ~ *Selah*

> I breathe in Divine Awareness to share the empowering gifts of forgiveness toward myself and others.

> Breathing out, I embrace inspired thinking, Divine Awareness.

Revenge: Meditation 3

Dear Revenge, have you no dignity?
Where are your clothes? ~ Selah

I breathe in Divine Awareness to
share the empowering gifts of
forgiveness toward myself and
others.

Breathing out, I protect others
with my inspired thinking, Divine
Awareness.

Revenge: Meditation 4

Dear Revenge, have you no dignity?
Where is your shelter? ~ Selah

I breathe in Divine Awareness to
share the empowering gifts of
forgiveness toward myself and
others.

Breathing out, I embrace inspired
thinking, Divine Awareness.

Revenge: Meditation 5

Dear Revenge, have you no dignity?
Where is your wealth? ~ Selah

I breathe in Divine Awareness to
share the empowering gifts of
forgiveness toward myself and
others.

Breathing out, I protect others
with my inspired thinking, Divine
Awareness.

Revenge: Meditation 6

Dear Revenge, have you no dignity?
Where is your nourishment? ~ *Selah*

I breathe in Divine Awareness to
share the empowering gifts of
forgiveness toward myself and
others.

Breathing out, I embrace inspired
thinking, Divine Awareness.

Meditations on Fairness

Science and religion suggest that time and distance are illusions of the mind. Think of [Quantum Entanglement] and [Eternity], respectively.

Our intentional thoughts, Divine Awareness, heal us and those around us, regardless of time or space. God's Divine Awareness and Tree of Life will heal those no longer with us.

In our relationship with Divine Awareness, and self-reflection, we imagine someone we can support who suffered from unfairness during their lifetime. We imagine a person we can pray for so their healing process will begin.

During our daily meditation, we use the language of Divine Awareness, kindness, and encouragement, and we begin to express those qualities in our daily lives.

We create only one meditation per day, lest we overindulge.

Fairness: Meditation 1

Dear Family and Friends, in my iniquity, I treated you unfairly; I bullied you. ~ Selah

I breathe in Divine Awareness to share the gift of forgiveness with others.

Breathing out, I protect others with my inspired thinking, Divine Awareness.

Fairness: Meditation 2

Dear Family and Friends, I offer amends where my unfair behavior has caused harm to you. ~ *Selah*

I breathe in Divine Awareness to share the gift of harmony with others.

Breathing out, I embrace inspired thinking, Divine Awareness.

Fairness: Meditation 3

Dear Family and Friends, I am here to make amends where you were unsettled and afraid of my unfair actions. ~ *Selah*

I breathe in the Divine Awareness to make amends to myself and others.

Breathing out, I protect myself and others with inspired thinking, Divine Awareness.

Fairness: Meditation 4

Dear Family and Friends, I offer tranquility, where Divine Awareness changed my outlook on life. ~ *Selah*

I breathe in Divine Awareness to share the gift of tranquility with others.

Breathing out, I embrace inspired thinking, Divine Awareness.

Fairness: Meditation 5

Dear Unfairness to others, you exist in each cell of my body. What can I do with you? ~ *Selah*

I breathe in Divine Awareness to share the gift of fairness with others.

Breathing out, I let unfairness float away like a leaf on the river.

Fairness: Meditation 6

Divine Awareness, you exist wherever I cast my eyes. Do you exist in my behavior toward myself and others? ~ *Selah*

I breathe in Divine Awareness to share the gift of empowering thoughts and actions with others.

Breathing out, I protect others with my inspired thinking, Divine Awareness.

Fairness: Meditation 7

Dear Unfairness to others, you exist in the form of misogyny. Do you exist in me? ~ *Selah*

Searching myself for negative self-talk, I breathe in.

Breathing out, I let negative self-talk float away from me like leaves on the river.

Fairness: Meditation 8

Dear Unfairness, you exist in the form of racism. Do you exist in me? ~ *Selah*

Searching myself for negative self-talk, I breathe in.

Breathing out, I let negative self-talk float away from me like leaves on the river.

Fairness: Meditation 9

Dear Unfairness, you exist in the form of bigotry. Do you exist in me? ~ *Selah*

Searching myself for negative self-talk, I breathe in.

Breathing out, I let negative self-talk float away from me like leaves on the river.

Fairness: Meditation 10

Dear Children, I have treated you unfairly. What can I do to make you whole? ~ *Selah*

I breathe in Divine Awareness to share the gift of amends with others.

Breathing out, I embrace inspired thinking, Divine Awareness.

Fairness: Meditation 11

Dear Unfairness, you exist at the table where my name goes unspoken, although I am seated with you. ~ *Divine Awareness*

I breathe in, aware of the gifts of Divine Awareness.

Breathing out, I protect others with my inspired thinking, Divine Awareness.

Fairness: Meditation 12

Dear Unfairness, you exist in the workplace where my name remains unspoken, although I labor alongside you. ~ *Divine Awareness*

I breathe in the Divine Awareness of inspired thoughts and actions in all areas of my life.

Breathing out, I embrace inspired thinking, Divine Awareness.

Fairness: Meditation 13

Dear Unfairness, you exist where my talents are unappreciated. ~ *Divine Awareness*

I breathe in, aware of the omnipotence of Divine Awareness.

Breathing out, I protect others with my inspired thinking, Divine Awareness.

Fairness: Meditation 14

Dear Unfairness, you exist where a few are powerful, and many are powerless. ~ *Divine Awareness*

Aware of the empowering gifts of lifting up each other, I breathe in.

Breathing out, I embrace inspired thinking, Divine Awareness.

Fairness: Meditation 15

Dear Family, I am here to restore the peace I stole from you in my iniquity. ~ *Selah*

I breathe in Divine Awareness to share the empowering gift of amends toward myself and others.

Breathing out, I protect others with my inspired thinking, Divine Awareness.

Fairness: Meditation 16

Divine Awareness forgave Humanity for her shortcomings and excesses. ~ *Divine Awareness*

I breathe in Divine Awareness, knowing I am not alone in my journey.

Breathing out, I embrace inspired thinking, Divine Awareness.

Meditations on Bullies

Bullies shackle themselves with secret thoughts; they feel alone in their suffering. Bullies are unsafe toward others because of their secret thoughts. Bullies are unnerved by the possibility that their secret thoughts might be known to others. In their self-reliance, bullies protect their secret thoughts at all costs, and they lead a double life.

During meditation, we realize the importance of sharing our secret thoughts with a trusted friend. We feel a sense of urgency to do this so that our connection with Divine Awareness will deepen. We become willing to share our thoughts to benefit others, and they do the same for others. We release the tension of secret thoughts by sharing them with a trusted friend.

We become safe people enveloped in a relationship with Divine Awareness to share our life stories with others. We become people with whom others feel safe spending their time.

In the following meditations, we speak the language of Divine Awareness, kindness, and encouragement and begin to express ourselves with those qualities in our daily lives.

We create only one meditation per day, lest we overindulge.

Bullies: Meditation 1

Dear Self-centeredness, you exist wherever I see a bully. ~ *Selah*

Embracing my self-awareness, I breathe in.

Breathing out, I let self-centeredness float away from me like leaves on the river.

Bullies: Meditation 2

Dear Bullies, what motivates you, if not your desire for food, shelter, physical safety, and material well-being? ~ *Selah*

Aware of life's bullies, I breathe in.

Breathing out, I let life's bullies float away from me like leaves on the river.

Bullies: Meditation 3

Dear Bullies, your self-pleasuring has no limit in its depravity. ~ *Selah*

Aware of the depths of the bully's self-centeredness and fear, I breathe in.

Breathing out, I let life's bullies float away from me like leaves on the river.

Bullies: Meditation 4

Divine Awareness, do you see my suffering? ~ *Bully*

I breathe in Divine Awareness to share the empowering gifts of compassion toward myself and others.

Breathing out, I protect others with my inspired thinking, Divine Awareness.

Bullies: Meditation 5

Divine Awareness, do you see my weakness? ~ *Bully*

I breathe in Divine Awareness to share the empowering gifts of humility toward myself and others.

Breathing out, I embrace inspired thinking, Divine Awareness.

Bullies: Meditation 6

Divine Awareness, do you see my fear-based thinking? ~ *Bully*

I breathe in Divine Awareness to share the empowering gifts of humility toward myself and others.

Breathing out, I protect others
with my inspired thinking, Divine
Awareness.

Bullies: Meditation 7

Divine Awareness, do you see my self-
reliance? ~ *Bully*

> I breathe in Divine Awareness to
> share the empowering gifts of
> humility toward myself and
> others.

> Breathing out, I embrace inspired
> thinking, Divine Awareness.

Bullies: Meditation 8

Dear Ego-self, you arrived in the form
of compassion, where I am suffering. ~
Bully

> I breathe in Divine Awareness to
> share the empowering gifts of
> compassion toward myself and
> others.

> Breathing out, I protect others
> with my inspired thinking, Divine
> Awareness.

Bullies: Meditation 9

Divine Awareness, you arrived in the
form of understanding, where I sought
to be understood. ~ *Bully*

> I breathe in Divine Awareness to
> share the empowering gift of
> understanding with others.

Breathing out, I embrace inspired thinking, Divine Awareness.

Bullies: Meditation 10

Divine Awareness, you arrived in the form of forgiveness, where I could no longer pay my debts. ~ *Bully*

I breathe in Divine Awareness to share the empowering gift of forgiveness with others.

Breathing out, I protect others with my inspired thinking, Divine Awareness.

Bullies: Meditation 11

Dear Ego-self, Divine Awareness gifts are your best solution when the elephant bully visits you. ~ *Selah*

I breathe in Divine Awareness to share the gifts of empowering thoughts and actions toward myself and others.

Breathing out, I embrace inspired thinking, Divine Awareness.

Bullies: Meditation 12

Dear Harmony, you manifested yourself from within the Ego-self. I am pleased with you. ~ *Divine Awareness*

I breathe in Divine Awareness to share the empowering gift of

harmony between myself and
others.

Breathing out, I protect others
with my inspired thinking, Divine
Awareness.

Meditations on Children

When a parent bullies us, the actor is their unhealed inner child. We did not realize our parent's inner child was bullying us. Instead, we assumed ourselves to be undeserving of their love and physical protection. Enduring this daily trauma, we believed ourselves to be unwanted and defective. As a result, we developed an internal bully with low self-esteem and negative self-talk, and we developed coping skills that may be our Achilles heal in adulthood and our relationship with others.

To overcome a parent bully, we approach the situation with prayer, meditation, and communication with others.

We share our suffering with a trusted friend and pray for Divine Awareness to heal someone who suffered this way. Praying for someone else begins to heal our self-worth and our self-esteem. With enough prayer, meditation, and communication with others, we are fulfilled, inspired, calm, and engaged in life.

We imagine ourselves and our parents when they were small children.

We imagine the selfish and the self-centered bully as if they are a small, determined child. We imagine each child suffering and reach out to that child with love and understanding. We reach out to each child with compassion. We reach out to each child with patience and humility. We reach out to each child with forgiveness and kindness.

We do not approve of the bully's actions. We understand the child within the bully, the child within ourselves.

In the following meditations, we speak the language of Divine Awareness, kindness, and encouragement and begin to express ourselves with those qualities in our daily lives.

We create only one meditation per day, lest we overindulge.

Children: Meditation 1

Dear Children, you are bitter and relentless. What can I do to make you whole? ~ *Selah*

I breathe in Divine Awareness to share the empowering gift of compassion toward myself and others.

Breathing out, I embrace inspired thinking, Divine Awareness.

Children: *Meditation 2*
Dear Children, you bring compassion, understanding, patience, and humility to those who say you are unworthy. ~ *Selah*

Aware of the resilience of children and their natural kindness, I breathe in.

Breathing out, I smile.

Children: *Meditation 3*
Dear Children, I receive your gifts of compassion. ~ *Selah*

I breathe in Divine Awareness to share the gifts of compassion I receive from others.

Breathing out, I smile.

Children: *Meditation 4*
Dear Children, I receive your gifts of playfulness. ~ *Selah*

I breathe in Divine Awareness to share the gifts of playfulness I receive from others.

Breathing out, I am grateful.

Meditations on Adults

While praying for ourselves and others, we create our prayers or rely on other prayers and meditations. We pray the prayers for ourselves, and we pray for someone else.

In the following meditations, we speak the language of Divine Awareness, kindness, and encouragement and begin to express ourselves with those qualities in our daily lives.

We create only one meditation per day, lest we overindulge.

Adult-Aged Children: Meditation 1
I choose to have loving conversations with my family. ~ *Selah*

> I breathe in Divine Awareness to share the empowering gift of kindness toward myself and others.

> Breathing out, I protect others with my inspired thinking, Divine Awareness.

Adult-Aged Children: Meditation 2
I choose to have loving conversations with my mother. ~ *Selah*

I breathe in Divine Awareness to
share the empowering gift of
kindness toward myself and
others.

Breathing out, I embrace
gratitude.

Adult-Aged Children: Meditation 3
I choose to share loving activities with
my family. ~ *Selah*

I breathe in Divine Awareness to
share the empowering gift of
kindness toward myself and
others.

Breathing out, I embrace
happiness.

Adult-Aged Children: Meditation 4
I choose to share loving activities with
my mother. ~ *Selah*

I breathe in Divine Awareness to
share the empowering gift of
kindness toward myself and
others.

Breathing out, I embrace
happiness.

Adult-Aged Children: Meditation 5
I suffered when avoiding conversations
with others. ~ *Selah*

I breathe in Divine Awareness to share the empowering gift of kindness toward myself and others.

Breathing out, I embrace happiness.

Adult-Aged Children: Meditation 6
I suffer by avoiding activities with others. ~ *Selah*

I breathe in Divine Awareness to share the empowering gift of kindness toward myself and others.

Breathing out, I embrace happiness.

Meditations on Ego-Self

Praying for others and meditating on someone else's well-being allows me to get out of my "cheap self" momentarily. Humanity provides countless opportunities to pray for someone else.

In the following meditations, we speak the language of Divine Awareness, kindness, and encouragement and begin to express ourselves with those qualities in our daily lives.

We create only one meditation per day, lest we overindulge.

Ego-Self: Meditation 1

Dear Humanity, you arrived wearing a sackcloth, covered in ashes. Welcome! Let me guide you to a better life. ~ *Divine Awareness*

> I breathe in Divine Awareness to share the empowering gift of compassion toward myself and others.
>
> Breathing out, I embrace inspired thinking, Divine Awareness.

Ego-Self: Meditation 2

Dear Humanity, you came to me, wounded and afraid. Would you like me to help you? ~ *Divine Awareness*

Aware of my compassion for those who are suffering, I breathe in.

Breathing out, I embrace inspired thinking, Divine Awareness.

Ego-Self: Meditation 3

Dear Humanity, are you hiding something from yourself and others? Are you willing to tell me about it? I may have had the same experience as you. ~ *Divine Awareness*

Aware of those who suffer in silence, I breathe in.

Breathing out, I encourage others to speak their truth.

Ego-Self: Meditation 4

Divine Awareness gives me the strength to embrace the self-reliant and the self-centered when they arrive wounded, bruised, and afraid. ~ *Humanity*

Aware of others who are lonely and afraid, I breathe in.

Breathing out, I encourage others to embrace our paths of Divine Awareness.

Ego-Self: Meditation 5

Divine Awareness, make me a channel of thy peace so that I can understand others where they seek to be understood. ~ *Humanity*

> I breathe in Divine Awareness to share the empowering gift of understanding with others.

> Breathing out, I am patient with myself and others.

Ego-Self: Meditation 6

Dear Humanity, you arrived in the form of unsettledness. Would you like me to help you? ~ *Divine Awareness*

> I breathe in Divine Awareness to share the empowering gift of helpfulness toward myself and others.

> Breathing out, I offer harmony where others are in discord.

Ego-Self: Meditation 7

Dear Humanity, you arrived mindfully seeking engagement through prayer and meditation. Please join me in the conversation so that I may know you better. ~ *Divine Awareness*

> I breathe in, aware of my gift of encouragement to those seeking Divine Awareness.

Breathing out, I encourage myself and others on our paths of healing.

Ego-Self: Meditation 8

Divine Awareness, you arrived in the form of understanding. Welcome to our conversation. I want to know you better. ~ *Selah*

I breathe in Divine Awareness to share the empowering gift of understanding with others.

Breathing out, I understand others where they seek to be understood.

Ego-Self: Meditation 9

Divine Awareness, you arrived in the form of compassion. Welcome to our conversation. I want to know you better. ~ *Selah*

I breathe in Divine Awareness to share the empowering gift of compassion toward myself and others.

Breathing out, I am compassionate toward those who suffer.

Ego-Self: Meditation 10

Divine Awareness, you arrived in the form of patience. Welcome to our conversation. I want to know you better. ~ *Selah*

110

I breathe in Divine Awareness to
share the empowering gift of
patience with others.

Breathing out, I am patient with
myself and others.

Ego-Self: Meditation 11
Dear Humanity, the diaspora caused
you harm. I understand your suffering.
I offer compassion to you. ~ *Divine
Awareness*

I breathe in Divine Awareness to
share the empowering gift of
compassion toward myself and
others.

Breathing out, I am
compassionate toward myself
and others.

Ego-Self: Meditation 12
Dear Humanity, you built great cities to
glorify yourself. I forgive you. I offer
compassion to you. ~ *Divine Awareness*

I breathe in Divine Awareness to
share the empowering gift of
humility toward myself and
others.

Breathing out, I am humbled.

Ego-Self: Meditation 13
Dear Humanity, I am here to make
amends and to replace what I stole

from you when I relied on self-centeredness. ~ *Selah*

> I breathe in Divine Awareness to share the empowering gift of forgiveness with others.

> Breathing out, I embrace inspired thinking, Divine Awareness.

Ego-Self: Meditation 14

Divine Awareness, I am here to pay restitution for your unsettledness with me. How can I make you whole? ~ *Selah*

> I breathe in Divine Awareness to share the empowering gift of forgiveness with others.

> Breathing out, I protect others with my inspired thinking, Divine Awareness.

Ego-Self: Meditation 15

Dear Humanity, I gave you the empowering character traits of compassion, understanding, patience, and humility. When will you pick up these tools and apply them to your lives? ~ *Divine Awareness*

> I breathe in Divine Awareness to share the gifts of empowering thoughts and actions toward myself and others.

Breathing out, I try again.

Ego-Self: Meditation 16

Dear Humanity, you have embraced my empowering character traits of patience and humility. Please, hold my hand as we walk together in life. ~ *Divine Awareness*

I breathe in Divine Awareness to share the empowering principle of grace with all who ask for it.

Breathing out, I am grateful.

Ego-Self: Meditation 17

Dear Humanity, I am here to celebrate our relationship. ~ *Divine Awareness*

I breathe, aware of new energy flowing through my body and mind.

Breathing out, I celebrate with others.

Meditations on Self-Reliance

Empowered by our relationship with Divine Awareness, we imagine a person we can pray for who may be suffering from self-reliance. We imagine a person we can pray for so their healing process will begin.

In the following meditations, we speak the language of Divine Awareness, kindness, and encouragement and begin to express ourselves with those qualities in our daily lives.

We create only one meditation per day, lest we overindulge.

Self-Reliance: Meditation 1

Dear God, I am powerless over the character trait of self-reliance, and my life is unmanageable. ~ *Selah*

I breathe in Divine Awareness to share the empowering gift of humility toward myself and others.

Breathing out, I embrace inspired thinking, Divine Awareness.

Self-Reliance: Meditation 2

Dear Ego-self, you tried your best to remain self-reliant. Are you willing to change? ~ *Divine Awareness*

114

I breathe in Divine Awareness to
share the empowering gift of
humility toward myself and
others.

Breathing out, I let self-reliance
float away from me like a leaf on
the river.

Self-Reliance: Meditation 3

Dear Self-reliance, you live among
thieves, despair, and bewilderment.
Please, hold my hand while we walk
together and find a solution. ~ *Divine
Awareness*

I breathe in the gifts of Divine
Awareness and overcome all
obstacles.

Breathing out, I protect others
with my inspired thinking, Divine
Awareness.

Self-Reliance: Meditation 4

Dear Higher Power, Self-reliance
seduced me and took my joy, my
happiness. Will you help me? ~ *Selah*

Aware of the empowering gift of
self-awareness, I breathe in.

Breathing out, I embrace inspired
thinking, Divine Awareness.

Self-Reliance: Meditation 5

Dear Ego-self, you play the role of a victim. Are you now willing to trust me and let go of that character flaw? ~ *Divine Awareness*

Aware of the empowering gift of self-awareness, I breathe in.

Breathing out, I protect others with my inspired thinking, Divine Awareness.

Self-Reliance: Meditation 6

Dear Self-reliance, you arrived with your friend, craving. Welcome to our conversation. I want to know you better. ~ *Divine Awareness*

Aware of the empowering gifts of self-awareness, I breathe in.

Breathing out, I embrace inspired thinking, Divine Awareness.

Self-Reliance: Meditation 7

Dear Self-reliance, you bully others and batter their kindness. ~ *Divine Awareness*

Aware of the empowering gift of self-awareness, I breathe in.

Breathing out, I offer the gifts of understanding and patience to myself and others.

Self-Reliance: Meditation 8

Dear Self-reliance, you exist in my bones, DNA, and chromosomes. May we now change course and embrace Divine Awareness? ~ *Selah*

Aware of the empowering gift of self-awareness, I breathe in.

Breathing out, I protect others with my kindness toward them.

Self-Reliance: Meditation 9

Dear Heaven, my character trait of self-reliance arrived with a rapacious creditor named fear. Please help me. ~ *A Self-Aware Person*

I breathe in Divine Awareness to share the empowering gift of understanding with others.

Breathing out, I offer my gift of acceptance to others.

Self-Reliance: Meditation 10

Dear Humanity, I am the fearmonger in your midst. ~ *Self-Reliance*

I breathe in Divine Awareness to share the empowering gift of understanding with others.

Breathing out, I embrace inspired thinking, Divine Awareness.

Self-Reliance: Meditation 11
Humility replaces the character trait of self-reliance. ~ *Divine Awareness*

Aware of my inspired way of living, I breathe in.

Breathing out, I am grateful.

Self-Reliance: Meditation 12
I understand self-reliance, where it seeks to be understood. ~ *Selah*

Aware of myself from an inspired point of view, I breathe in.

Breathing out, I protect others with my inspired thinking, Divine Awareness.

Self-Reliance: Meditation 13
I found patience, where self-reliance had been unstoppable in me. ~ *Selah*

Aware of myself from an inspired perspective, I breathe in.

Breathing out, I embrace inspired thinking, Divine Awareness.

Self-Reliance: Meditation 14
Dear humility, you caused me to let go of self-reliance. ~ *Selah*

I breathe in Divine Awareness to share the empowering gift of humility toward myself and others.

Breathing out, I protect others
with my inspired thinking, Divine
Awareness.

Meditations on Craving

In the following meditations, we speak the language of Divine Awareness, kindness, and encouragement and begin to express ourselves with those qualities in our daily lives.

We create only one meditation per day, lest we overindulge.

Craving: Meditation 1

Dear Ego-self, your need for social approval has no end. ~ *Divine Awareness*

> I breathe in Divine Awareness to share the empowering gift of acceptance toward myself and others.
>
> Breathing out, I offer gifts of acceptance to myself and others.

Craving: Meditation 2

Dear Ego-self, where you need compassion, understanding, patience, and humility, give all this to others, and these character strengths will come to you. ~ *Divine Awareness*

> I breathe in Divine Awareness to share the gifts of empowering actions toward myself and others.

Breathing out, I offer myself and others the gift of Divine Awareness.

Craving: Meditation 3

Dear Ego-self, having personal safety, joyful friendships, and material well-being would be best. ~ *Divine Awareness*

I breathe in, aware of the Divine Awareness in giving to others.

Breathing out, I offer my gift of personal safety to myself and others.

Meditations on Suicide Prevention

Call 988
(National Suicide Hotline)

"Anger is an acid that can do more harm to the vessel in which it is stored than to the object on which it is poured." —Lucius Annaeus Seneca (AD 65)

In the following meditations, we speak the language of Divine Awareness, kindness, and encouragement and begin to express ourselves with those qualities in our daily lives.

We create only one meditation per day, lest we overindulge.

Suicide Prevention: Meditation 1
Dear Ego-self, when I gave in to life's bullies, I decided that you were not important to me, which was a mistake on my part.

I am here now to make amends and to pay restitution to you for my lack of good judgment. ~ *Selah*

Aware of an inspired way of life, I breathe in.

Breathing out, I embrace
inspired thinking, Divine
Awareness.

Suicide Prevention: Meditation 2

Dear Humanity, I gave up on sharing
my joy for life with you as I thought you
did not hear or see me. I am here now
to transform my self-pity into the
outward flow of compassion,
understanding, patience, and humility
toward you. ~ *Selah*

I breathe in Divine Awareness to
share the gifts of compassion
toward myself and others.

Breathing out, I embrace inspired
thinking, Divine Awareness.

Suicide Prevention: Meditation 3

Divine Awareness, I gave up on sharing
my joy for life with you as I thought I
was not loved. I am here now to
transform my self-pity into the outward
flow of compassion, understanding,
patience, and humility toward you. ~
Selah

I breathe in Divine Awareness to
share the gifts of patience with
others.

Breathing out, I embrace inspired
thinking, Divine Awareness.

Suicide Prevention: Meditation 4

Dear Humanity, I realize you could do nothing to encourage my joy in life. For you, too, were imprisoned by bullies. ~ *Selah*

I breathe in Divine Awareness to share the gifts of understanding with others.

Breathing out, I embrace inspired thinking, Divine Awareness.

Suicide Prevention: Meditation 5

Dear Ego-self, I see an absent and abusive parent extinguished your hopes and dreams for a joyful life. Did you ask someone for help? ~ *Selah*

I breathe in Divine Awareness to share the gifts of compassion toward myself and others.

Breathing out, I embrace inspired thinking, Divine Awareness.

Suicide Prevention: Meditation 6

Dear Ego-self, in your isolation and fear, did you ask someone for help as you suffered? ~ *Selah*

I breathe in Divine Awareness to share the gifts of empowering thoughts and actions toward myself and others.

Breathing out, I embrace inspired thinking, Divine Awareness.

Suicide Prevention: Meditation 7
Dear Ego-self, when you encountered life's bullies, did you ask anyone for help as you suffered? ~ *Selah*

I breathe in Divine Awareness to share the gifts of empowering thoughts and actions toward myself and others.

Breathing out, I embrace inspired thinking, Divine Awareness.

Meditations on Forgiveness

Forgiveness: Meditation 1

Dear Resentment, my joy for life is unrequited by you. I choose not to poison myself with plans for revenge.

I forgive you, not because you deserve it, but because I deserve to be free of the negativity in my body, mind, and soul. ~ *Selah*

> I breathe in Divine Awareness to share the empowering gift of compassion toward myself and others.

> Breathing out, I let resentments float away like leaves on the river.

Forgiveness: Meditation 2

Dear Abusive family member, my joy for life is unrequited by you. I choose not to poison myself with resentment and revenge.

I forgive you, not because you deserve it, but because I deserve to be free of any negativity in my body, mind, and soul. ~ *Selah*

> I breathe in Divine Awareness to share the empowering gift of forgiveness with others.

126

Breathing out, I let resentments
float away like leaves on the river.

Forgiveness: Meditation 3

Dear Humanity, I receive your
forgiveness for my shortcomings. ~
Selah

I breathe in Divine Awareness to
share the gifts of empowering
thoughts and actions toward
myself and others.

Breathing out, I let shortcomings
float away from me like leaves on
the river.

Meditations on Amends

In the following meditations, we speak the language of Divine Awareness, kindness, and encouragement and begin to express ourselves with those qualities in our daily lives.

We create only one meditation per day, lest we overindulge.

Amends: Meditation 1

Dear Family and Friends, I withheld my joy from you in my iniquity. I wish to undo this harm to you. I wish to make amends and pay restitution to you. ~ *Selah*

I breathe in, aware of the Divine Awareness of making amends to myself and others.

Breathing out, I offer gifts of amends to myself and others.

Amends: Meditation 2

Dear Humanity, I withheld my joy from you in self-reliance. I wish to undo this harm to you. I wish to make amends and pay restitution to you. ~ *Selah*

I breathe in, aware of the Divine Awareness of making amends to myself and others.

Breathing out, I offer gifts of
amends to myself and others.

Amends: *Meditation 3*
Dear Ego-self, in the form of a five-
year-old child, I gave in to life's bullies
because I had no resources to protect
you at that age. I am here to make
amends and to pay restitution to you. ~
Selah

I breathe in, aware of the Divine
Awareness of making amends to
myself and others.

Breathing out, I offer gifts of
forgiveness to myself and others.

Amends: *Meditation 4*
Dear Family, I gave you no safe harbor
or compassion in my resentment and
mistrust of you as a child. I give you
my compassion, understanding,
patience, and humility as an adult. ~
Selah

I breathe in, aware of the Divine
Awareness of making amends to
myself and others.

Breathing out, I embrace inspired
thinking, Divine Awareness.

Meditations on Gratitude

I sought my soul,
But my soul I could not see.
I sought my God,
But my God eluded me.
I sought my brother,
and I found all three.
—William Blake (1757—1827)

In our life of Divine Awareness, we express our gratitude through the way we live, the way we speak, and the way we pray.

In the following meditations, we speak the language of Divine Awareness, kindness, and encouragement and begin to express ourselves with those qualities in our daily lives.

We create only one meditation per day, lest we overindulge.

Gratitude: Meditation 1
Dear Happiness, I found you in the form of a trusted friend. You were patient when I struggled to speak my truth. ~ *Selah*

I breathe in Divine Awareness to share the empowering gift of honesty with myself and others.

Breathing out, I am at peace.

130

Gratitude: Meditation 2

Dear Comfort, I found you in the form of a trusted friend. You forgave me when I plotted against you for my selfish purposes. ~ *Selah*

I breathe in Divine Awareness to share the empowering gift of forgiveness with others.

Breathing out, I protect others with my inspired thinking, Divine Awareness.

Gratitude: Meditation 3

Dear Encouragement, I found you in the form of a trusted friend. You understood me when I did not understand myself. ~ *Selah*

I breathe in Divine Awareness to share the gifts of understanding with others.

Breathing out, I embrace inspired thinking, Divine Awareness.

Gratitude: Meditation 4

Divine Awareness, I found you in the form of a trusted friend. You gave me compassion when I did not love myself. ~ *Selah*

I breathe in Divine Awareness to share the gifts of harmony and compassion toward myself and others.

Breathing out, I am blessed.

Gratitude: Meditation 5
Divine Awareness, I found you in the form of a trusted friend. You created harmony in me by listening to my story. ~ *Selah*

I breathe in, aware of new energy flowing through my mind and body.

Breathing out, I am at peace.

Part IV

Compassion

We are the caretaker of each other's peace of mind, yet we provoke each other by consuming the daily news, digesting, and regurgitating fear, hate, and mayhem.

Unconsciously, our Ego-self looks at itself in every person we contact and says, "I am suffering just like the Ego-self is suffering over there, within that person."

Our Ego-self does not differentiate between "us" and "them." The family dog, akin to our Ego-self, looks at you directly in the eyes and stares at you because it believes you see and care for its Divine Awareness just as clearly as it cares for yours. But Humanity makes this connection carefully— sometimes only if we think we will get something in return.

Note to self: Do better!

Prayers of Healing

Dear Ego-self, where you exist in my Garden of Eden, my Garden of Memories, I accept Divine Awareness as my amends for not knowing a better way to live, think and respond to adversity. ~ *Selah*

Dear Selah, where I have judged you harshly and abused you with alcohol and drugs, I accept Divine Awareness as my amends to you for not knowing a better way to live, think and respond to adversity. ~ *Selah*

Dear Inner Child, where I have fallen short of your expectations, I accept Divine Awareness as my amends to you for not knowing a better way to live, think and respond to adversity. ~ *Selah*

Divine Awareness, I am honored and humbled to know you exist in my DNA, chromosomes, and cells. ~ *Selah*

Divine Awareness, I know you are healing my sister in ways I cannot understand or comprehend. ~ *Selah*

Divine Awareness, I know you are healing my father of his worries, fears, and secret thoughts. ~ *Namaste`*

Dear Ego-self and Inner Child, where you see me as unworthy and a failure, I have become a blessing to myself and others with the help of Divine Awareness. ~ *Selah*

Dear Alcohol and Drugs, where you stole my sanguinity and ravaged my body, I have become a blessing to myself and others with the help of Divine Awareness. ~ *Selah*

Dear Captor, where you wanted to kill me, I have become a blessing to myself and others with the help of Divine Awareness. ~ *Selah*

Dear Enemies, Divine Awareness, is the blessing you seek. ~ *Selah*

Divine Awareness, you are the blessing I seek. ~ *Selah*

Divine Awareness, you are the blessing my family is seeking. ~ *Selah*

Divine Awareness, you are the blessing my children are seeking. ~ *Selah*

Breathwork

The advanced practitioner may want to research the Wim Hof breathing method and related YouTube videos, which are lovely and relaxing.

The Wim Hof breathing technique, also known as the "Wim Hof Method," is a type of breathing exercise designed to increase oxygen intake and energy levels while reducing stress and anxiety.

The technique consists of three phases:

Deep breathing: The first phase involves taking 30 deep breaths in succession, inhaling deeply through your nose, and exhaling through your mouth.

Breath retention: After the 30th breath, exhale fully and hold your breath for as long as possible; typically done for 1-2 minutes.

Recovery breath: After the breath retention phase, hold one deep breath for 10-15 seconds before exhaling, which is one round of the Wim Hof breathing technique.

This process can be repeated for several rounds, and the benefits of the technique include improved immune function, increased energy and focus, reduced inflammation, and improved mental clarity and emotional regulation.

It is important to note that while the Wim Hof breathing technique can be beneficial, it should not be done in water or while driving, and it is important to listen to your body and stop if you feel lightheaded or uncomfortable. It is also recommended to learn the technique from a qualified instructor.

Practice Sets

Divine Awareness, we are grateful to be with you in the Garden of Eden, the Garden of Memories, in the midst of the garden, knowing good and evil. ~ *Selah*

~

Divine Awareness, Tree of Life, you are the family we seek.
> *Breathing in, I know I am breathing in.*
> *Breathing out, I smile.*

~

Divine Awareness, you are the community we seek.
> *Breathing in, I know I am breathing in.*
> *Breathing out, I smile.*

~

Divine Awareness, Tree of Life, you are the happiness we seek.
> *Breathing in, I know I am breathing in.*
> *Breathing out, I smile.*

~

Divine Awareness, Tree of Life, you are the gratitude we seek.
Breathing in, I know I am breathing in.
Breathing out, I smile.

~

Divine Awareness, Tree of Life, you are the fairness we seek.
Breathing in, I know I am breathing in.
Breathing out, I smile.

~

Divine Awareness, Tree of Life, you are the forgiveness we seek.
Breathing in, I know I am breathing in.
Breathing out, I smile.

~

Divine Awareness, Tree of Life, you are the amends we seek to make.
Breathing in, I know I am breathing in.
Breathing out, I smile.

~

Divine Awareness, Tree of Life, you are the honesty we seek.
Breathing in, I know I am breathing in.
Breathing out, I smile.

~

Divine Awareness, Tree of Life, you are the truth we seek.
Breathing in, I know I am breathing in.
Breathing out, I smile.

~

Divine Awareness, Tree of Life, you are the patience we seek.
Breathing in, I know I am breathing in.
Breathing out, I smile.

~

Divine Awareness, Tree of Life, you are the humility we seek.
Breathing in, I know I am breathing in.
Breathing out, I smile.

~

Divine Awareness, Tree of Life, you are the harmony we seek.
Breathing in, I know I am breathing in.
Breathing out, I smile.

~

Divine Awareness, Tree of Life, you are the perseverance we seek.
Breathing in, I know I am breathing in.
Breathing out, I smile.

~

We Let Go

Inside each of us is an awareness of Divine Energy and Knowledge, or Divinity that is greater than us. The Divinity requires we "believe" or "claim" its existence rather than prove it exists. Similarly, Divinity requires that we claim our beliefs on a broader scale which we describe in this chapter and the next chapter.

In the following meditations, we speak the language of Divine Awareness, kindness, and encouragement and begin to express ourselves with those qualities in our daily lives.

We create only one meditation per day, lest we overindulge.

~

I am no longer codependent and wimpy ~ because I claim this truth and honor myself.

I am no longer inferior ~ because I claim this truth and honor myself.

I am no longer unwanted ~ because I claim this truth and honor myself.

I am no longer despised ~ because I claim this truth and honor myself.

I am no longer undesirable ~ because I claim this truth and honor myself.

I am no longer clinging and grasping ~ because I claim this truth and honor myself.

I am no longer a disappointment to myself or others ~ because I claim this truth and honor myself.

I no longer sabotage my relationships ~ because I claim this truth and honor myself.

I am no longer helpless and afraid ~ because I claim this truth and honor myself.

I am no longer alone and afraid ~ because I claim this truth and honor myself.

I no longer belittle myself ~ because I claim this truth and honor myself.

I no longer bully myself ~ because I claim this truth and honor myself.

I am no longer giving up ~ because I claim this truth and honor myself.

I am no longer plotting against others ~ because I claim this truth and honor myself.

I no longer hate myself ~ because I claim this truth and honor myself.

I am no longer isolating myself ~ because I claim this truth and honor myself.

I am no longer irrelevant ~ because I claim this truth and honor myself.

I am no longer giving up and overwhelmed ~ because I claim this truth and honor myself.

I am no longer ashamed of my family or place in society ~ because I claim this truth and honor myself.

I am no longer ashamed of myself ~ because I claim this truth and honor myself.

I am no longer ashamed of my substance abuse and addictions ~ because I claim this truth and honor myself.

I am no longer ashamed of my survival skills ~ because I claim this truth and honor myself.

I have no envy or rage ~ because I claim this truth and honor myself.

I am no longer sad or inferior ~ because I claim this truth and honor myself.

I am no longer anxious ~ because I claim this truth and honor myself.

I am no longer disappointed in life ~ because I claim this truth and honor myself.

I am no longer disappointed in myself ~ because I claim this truth and honor myself.

We Claim Our Truths

"Our minds are trained through millennia to repeat the familiar and to blend in with the rest of our tribe. To do otherwise would be certain death a few thousand years ago. Today, our minds struggle with the unfamiliar because of the energy requirement and genetic programming. Fortunately, neuroplasticity is on our side if we do the work of intentionally retraining our thought-life." Paraphrased from a Ted talk on Overcoming Trauma by *Gabor Maté.*

In the following meditations, we speak the language of Divine Awareness, kindness, and encouragement and begin to express ourselves with those qualities in our daily lives.

We create only one meditation per day, lest we overindulge.

~

I can and will overcome any obstacles ~ because I claim this truth and honor myself.

I am a good friend ~ because I claim this truth and honor myself.

I am compassionate, understanding, patient, and humble ~ because I claim this truth and honor myself.

I am accountable ~ because I claim this truth and honor myself.

I am a servant leader ~ because I claim this truth and honor myself.

I am a values-based leader ~ because I claim this truth and honor myself.

I am man enough ~ because I claim this truth and honor myself.

I am woman enough ~ because I claim this truth and honor myself.

I am sober ~ because I claim this truth and honor myself.

I am wealthy ~ because I claim this truth and honor myself.

I am likable ~ because I claim this truth and honor myself.

I am happy ~ because I claim this truth and honor myself.

I am healthy ~ because I claim this truth and honor myself.

My bones are healthy and thriving ~ because I claim this truth and honor myself.

My organs are healthy and thriving ~ because I claim this truth and honor myself.

My eyes are healthy and thriving ~ because I claim this truth and honor myself.

My hair and nails are healthy and thriving ~ because I claim this truth and honor myself.

My fingers and toes are healthy and thriving ~ because I claim this truth and honor myself.

My skin and muscles are healthy and thriving ~ because I claim this truth and honor myself.

I have no fear of people ~ because I claim this truth and honor myself.

I do not fear economic insecurity ~ because I claim this truth and honor myself.

I have no fear of failure ~ because I claim this truth and honor myself.

I have no fear of hardships ~ because I claim this truth and honor myself.

My words are authentic ~ because I claim this truth and honor myself.

My testimony is credible ~ because I claim this truth and honor myself.

My work product is exemplary ~ because I claim this truth and honor myself.

I am artistic ~ because I claim this truth and honor myself.

I am intelligent ~ because I claim this truth and honor myself.

I am physically talented ~ because I claim this truth and honor myself.

My thoughts are healthy ~ because I claim this truth and honor myself.

My smile is genuine ~ because I claim this truth and honor myself.

I am a gift to others ~ because I claim this truth and honor myself.

Others celebrate me ~ because I claim this truth and honor myself.

My emotions are necessary and authentic ~ because I claim this truth and honor myself.

I make friends easily ~ because I claim this truth and honor myself.

I am confident ~ because I claim this truth and honor myself.

I am competent ~ because I claim this truth and honor myself.

I trust myself ~ because I claim this truth and honor myself.

I am a fast learner ~ because I claim this truth and honor myself.

I have an excellent memory ~ because I claim this truth and honor myself.

I am wealthy ~ because I claim this truth and honor myself.

I care about others ~ because I claim this truth and honor myself.

I am helpful to others ~ because I claim this truth and honor myself.

I am a good parent ~ because I claim this truth and honor myself.

I am a great public speaker ~ because I claim this truth and honor myself.

I am entertaining to be with ~ because I claim this truth and honor myself.

Divine Awareness is alive in me ~ because I claim this truth and honor myself.

סְ.לִ.יחָ.ה

Divine Awareness, I accept you as my amends for not knowing a better way to live, thrive, or respond to adversities. ~ *Selah*

Divine Awareness, I accept your healing grace. I have no claim against you. I am at peace. ~ *Selah*

סוּפִי

Extra Reading

The Soul of Shame: Retelling the Stories We Believe About Ourselves by Curt Thompson

John E. Sarno, M.D - The Mind Body Prescription: Healing the Body, Healing the Pain

Thich Nhat Hahn - Plum Village Meditations

Thich Nhat Hahn - Body and Mind Are One, A Training in Mindfulness

Breathing Under Water: Spirituality and the Twelve Steps https://a.co/d/bHn8jr9

Ryan Holiday - The Obstacle is the Way: The Timeless Art of Turning Trials into Triumph

Lezlie Laws – TIA Journal (Thank-Intend-Ask Journal)

Blue Letter Bible

Health Benefits of Prayer

Healing through Prayer

Prayer is a special form of meditation and may convey all the health benefits of meditation.

Different types of meditation have been shown to result in psychological and biological changes that are actually or potentially associated with improved health. Meditation can reduce blood pressure and heart rate, boost the immune response, reduce anxiety and pain, and enhance self-esteem.

Meditation is known to favorably influence a person's quality of Life in late-stage disease, improvement in a positive mood, and tolerance to pain. — *Indian Journal of Psychiatry*

Placebo Effect of Prayer

Supported by varying degrees of faith, prayer may be associated with all the benefits of the placebo response. Spontaneous remission occurs in conditions ranging from medical disorders to psychiatric states. —*Indian Journal of Psychiatry*

Types of Prayer

Christian Prayer
Prayer, meditation, and contemplation in Christianity are integral elements of the Christian faith and permeate all forms of Christian worship. Prayer in Christianity is the tradition of communicating with God, either in God's fullness or as one of the persons of the Trinity (via Wikipedia).

Affirmative Prayer
An affirmative prayer is a form of prayer or a metaphysical technique focused on a positive outcome rather than a negative situation (via Wikipedia).

Centering Prayer
A method of meditation used by Christians places a strong emphasis on interior silence. Thomas Merton described contemplative prayer (a much older and more traditional practice) as a prayer that is "centered entirely on the presence of God" (via Wikipedia).

Types of Meditation

Mindfulness Meditation

Mindfulness is the psychological process of bringing one's attention to shares occurring in the present moment, which one can develop through meditation and other training (via Wikipedia).

Buddhism refers to mindfulness meditation as Vipassana; Insight is a clear awareness of exactly what is happening as it happens (via Wikipedia).

Metta Meditation

Mettā or maitrī means benevolence, loving-kindness, friendliness, amity, goodwill, and active interest in others.

Buddhism refers to Metta meditation as Samatha, concentration, and tranquility (via Wikipedia).

Meditating with Kids

The Greater Good Science Center studies well-being psychology, sociology, and neuroscience and teaches skills that foster a thriving, resilient, compassionate society.

https://greatergood.berkeley.edu/article/item/better_than_sex_and_appropriate_for_kids

Tonglen Meditation

In practice, one visualizes taking in the suffering of oneself and others on the in-breath and the out-breath, giving recognition, compassion, and assistance to all sentient beings. As such, it is training in altruism (via Wikipedia).

Self-Compassion Meditation

https://self-compassion.org/guided-self-compassion-meditations-mp3-2/

"Fierce self-compassion involves taking action to protect, provide, and motivate ourselves to reduce our suffering. It means saying "no" to others hurting us—drawing our boundaries firmly — or saying "no" to our harmful behaviors to be safe and healthy. It means giving ourselves what we genuinely need—mentally, emotionally, physically—without subordinating our needs to others so that we can be authentic and fulfilled." — Dr. Kristen Neff.

Afterword

Selah welcomes your feedback. To take part in this book, please write to Editor@Hannity-Press.com.

This book is available now on Amazon and Kindle. Coming soon to Audible.com

Made in United States
Orlando, FL
17 December 2023

41260450R00085